Taming Teenage Anxiety with ACT

The Six Core Processes of ACT That Help Parents Understand Their Teenager's Battle Against Social Media Anxiety and Thoughts of Self-Harm

Lillian Middleton

By Lillian Middleton

IMPORTANT MESSAGE: This book is intended to provide useful information on the subject matter contained within. It is for informational and entertainment purposes only, is not intended, and should not be used as a substitute for professional medical, psychological, financial, legal, or other advice, diagnosis, or treatment. The author is not diagnosing conditions or offering medical or mental health advice. The information in this book is NOT intended to be used for self-diagnosis or treatment. Before you change your health routine or start any diet, you should contact your doctor. Neither the publisher nor the author shall be held liable or responsible for any loss or damage allegedly arising from any suggestion or information contained in this book.

While the interview is based on the experiences of an actual individual, the name and personal characteristics of this person have been altered to preserve the privacy of the individual.

If you feel you require immediate help, please contact the appropriate authorities, medical providers, and/or crisis intervention service providers in your local area for immediate assistance.

Contents

Introduction vii

1. The Anxiety Epidemic: Unraveling the Threads of Teenage Worries 1
2. Reaching Radical Resilience: The Transformative Power of ACT for Teens 6
3. Voices of Resilience: Teenagers Speak Out on Battling Anxiety 16
4. When the World Stands Still: Navigating Teenage Anxiety Amidst the COVID-19 Pandemic 38
5. The Social Dilemma: Establishing Social Media's Impact on Teenage Anxiety 54
6. Breaking the Silence: Understanding Teenage Anxiety, Suicide, and Self-Harm 69
7. Guiding Through the Storm: Parenting Teenagers with Anxiety 92

Embracing Resilience: Thriving Beyond Teenage Anxiety 103

Bibliography 109

Introduction

Anxiety is defined by the Oxford Dictionary as "A feeling of worry, nervousness, or unease, usually about an impending event or something with an uncertain outcome."

Although the definition is clear and concise, the experience of unease is complex. The foundation of the sufferer's very existence feels torn apart. Anxiety is different for everyone and can manifest in many forms. Some people experience anxiety on a mild scale. These people can function normally. They can focus on daily tasks and be productive. Anxiety exists more like a song playing in the back of their heads. The person may not even notice anxious periods. Mild anxiety is something everyone faces, and it passes like a cloud on an otherwise sunny day.

However, as you place more weight on the anxiety scale, it moves into the forefront of your mind. It pushes and bullies itself there, spreading insidiously until it shrouds every thought with worry and dread. Those thoughts are negative - heavy and deadly like pelted stones. They shatter the fragile glass of your heart. The pain in your chest makes every breath a struggle. This impending thing – something you might not even be able to identify or name – is coming straight at you like a bullet train at full speed.

Your body feels the blows of your attacking mind. There are so many aches. Stomach aches. Headaches. Muscle aches. It is hard to wake up to such melancholy day after day because this is not a one-off occurrence. It is almost constant. It feels easier to stay in bed all day. To hide away from friends, family, and the many triggers that make the mental rocks larger. It might not even feel like you have a choice since your limbs feel so heavy, the light is too bright for your eyes, and the sounds of everyday life are like a gong ringing in your ears.

This description sounds like a dark tale written by the Brothers Grimm, right? But for the almost 32 percent of teens in the US who endure the symptoms of an anxiety disorder, this is the reality many live through.

Many teens hide these symptoms because they feel no one understands their agony. Truthfully, not many people do understand. These teens must open up about their illness because anxiety is a real-life sickness that needs attention, care, and treatment. Anxiety is agonizing and debilitating. You can never recover the parts of your day anxiety steals. When gripped in the throes of an anxiety attack, it can seem like there is no way out, especially when treatments are inaccessible.

Life is not an easy road to walk when anxiety is a companion every step of the way— nagging, prodding, and twisting itself around every encounter or incident. Your teen certainly has a turbulent journey ahead. There is also a certain amount of grief in knowing your child must fight so hard to live life happily. Many parents would sacrifice a limb to take away even the most minuscule pain or discomfort their child feels. It is disheartening to know you cannot take this affliction away. It breaks your heart to know your child lacks the confidence to grab life by the horns because of fears you cannot see. Knowing that anxiety affects academics, sports, and extracurricular performances hurts. Your family dynamic suffers due to anger, outbursts, and social withdrawal. The situation might seem hopeless — like this will never change or improve.

This book debunks that myth. There is hope! While the parents of a teen with anxiety cannot take this pain away, you can help them counter the rainy days by introducing them to coping skills so they can overcome those anxiety symptoms and live a fulfilling life full of joy and happiness. Anxiety does not go away. However, one can manage it and bring it down to mild or moderate levels, allowing it to the weight of a metaphorical fanny pack around your teen's waist versus a backpack full of rocks. I can tell you this with certainty because I know what it's like to be on both sides of the fence. I was a teen with anxiety, and now I am the parent of a teenage daughter with anxiety.

Has my anxiety gone away over the past years? No, it has not. But anxiety no longer controls my day or the things I do. I do get out of bed every day and go at life hard, something I did not think I could do as a teen with incapacitating anxiety. I have gone through almost every therapy and exercised virtually every coping skill under the sun to manage my anxiety. I have gone the formal route and seen licensed mental health professionals. I have also practiced relaxation techniques that can be done alone and without professional guidance. Some aided me, and some did not, but I have pulled something valuable from every one of them.

There was no magic cure for my anxiety, but I can confidently say my negative thoughts no longer frame my view of the world. I use all I have learned over the years to take my mind back as my own and live life how I want to and not how anxious thoughts dictate I should. My daughter also benefits from my experiences. She lives a typical teenage life rather than being socially withdrawn, isolated, or underfunctioning. In the coming pages, I will bestow on you the same lessons I taught her.

Introduction

I am not a psychologist or a psychiatrist, so I will not communicate with you like I am one. Instead, you will find my personal experiences and lessons learned delivered in everyday, easy-to-understand language. As mentioned in our previous book, my closest friend is a licensed psychiatrist who provided consultation on this current project. This collaboration significantly enhances the book's credibility and knowledge base.

Your teen can develop the coping skills needed to overcome the symptoms of anxiety. This book contains information on therapies like Acceptance and Commitment Therapy (ACT) and how to help an anxious mind navigate a world highly ruled by social media and recovering from a pandemic. It also spotlights the suicidal ideation of teenagers whose painful psyches cause extremely debilitating and intrusive thoughts, as well as those who have or might practice self-harm. You can't shoulder the burden of anxiety for your teen, but you can help them and your entire family better manage the symptoms to create a well-rounded life.

Teenagers are on the cusp of adulthood. They are learning about themselves, the wider world, and how they – with their unique abilities, insights, and perspectives – fit into this world. That is a challenging task, and it is only made more complicated and confusing by fighting an invisible monster dwelling within. Unfortunately, 1 in 3 teenagers in the US is fighting this beast, and if the brute is not tamed, it can lead to the teen having ideas of self-harm. Even worse, these ideas can be turned into action.

Suicide was "the second-leading cause of death among 10- to 24-year-olds" in 2018 in the US. A 2019 *Youth Behavioral Risk Factor Surveillance System* showed that almost 19 percent of high school students in the US seriously considered dying by suicide. According to the National Alliance on Mental Illness, 8.9 percent of adolescents attempted the fatal act.

Such statistics are distressing. Even more painful is how many of those teens succeeded in their attempts. We must do all we can to prevent teens from extinguishing their light prematurely.

Suicide is preventable.

The fact that these teens thought they had no other way out shows that more education is needed. More people need to know resources are available to alleviate anxiety symptoms. They do not have to be expensive, either. This book is one such resource.

The *National Suicide* and *Crisis Lifeline* also provides an invaluable aid through a listening ear. Just dial or text 988. If you, your teen, or anyone else you know is experiencing self-harm or suicidal thoughts, call the suicide hotline (988) or 911 or 999.

You are not alone in this struggle, and neither is your teen, as long as they have someone who cares about them as much as you do. Let this book be a friend to both of you. I encourage you to read this book with your teen. Get them a copy of their own so they can keep private notes and reminders to themselves.

To benefit from this book, you must do two things:

1. Be receptive to new ideas and healing.
2. Act on the given information.

Both you and your teen have suffered trauma from anxiety. Healing needs to take place for you two to find peace. No matter how effective a therapy or coping skill is, it will be useless to either of you if your heart and mind are not open to healing and considering new ideas and points of view.

They will also not be effective if you two do not put in work to make daily life not just survivable for your teen but also a time where they thrive mentally and emotionally.

I hope this and my other book, *Taming Teenage Anxiety with CBT and DBT*, also available on Amazon, helps as many anxious teens and their families as possible. Still, it is not a replacement for therapy, medication, or any other treatment a licensed mental health expert prescribes. Anxiety is a medical illness, and it is always best to seek the advice of a professional to manage it before it reaches extreme levels. This book can be a companion on that journey and even point you toward finding such aid.

Picture the person your teen can be. They can get out of bed with firm steps and participate in life with arms, hearts, and minds wide open. Hold that picture in your mind. Like a medallion over your heart, reach for it repeatedly as you read this book. Your and your teen's goal is to shake off the muck of anxiety and emerge like a butterfly from a cocoon, renewed and fluttering eagerly toward new horizons.

Turn the page to help your teen start that transformation.

Chapter 1
The Anxiety Epidemic: Unraveling the Threads of Teenage Worries

Research shows that between 2001 and 2004, almost one-third (31.9%) of the US adolescent population aged thirteen to eighteen years had an anxiety disorder. The age range of seventeen to eighteen years was affected the most. That number has only increased because of the COVID-19 pandemic, according to the *Centers for Disease Control and Prevention* (CDC). Data received in 2021 revealed that 37 percent of high school students in the US experienced a decline in mental health during the pandemic. Even more (44%) felt hopeless and sad simultaneously.

These teens have experienced lockdowns and social distancing like the rest of us. The pandemic disrupted education and daily routines. It robbed them of the social activities that brought joy and reprieve from daily stressors. They were isolated from friends and peers.

Life has slowly returned to normal as of 2022, but many youngsters are not rebounding well from the despair. Anxiety in adolescents was already on the rise before the COVID-19 pandemic. The virus only accelerated the rate.

The reasons for this rise vary. Teens are worried and feel pressured about their academic performance and choosing the right path into adulthood. Their bodies are changing: acne, weight gain or loss, growth spurts, body hair, hormones going haywire, and all the other changes that come with puberty. Teens are often unsettled in their skin. Social media and peer groups make them hypervigilant about how they are perceived, which only serves to compound these issues.

Anxiety - worry, unease, or nervousness is an everyday occurrence. However, when it persists and interferes with a person's normal functioning, it becomes a problem that needs addressing. Anxiety may be something your teenager grew up with. They may have been afraid of bugs, the dark, imagined monsters under their bed, or even something terrible happening to the people they love most, like their mom and dad. These are all external sources of anxiety. The source of teenage anxiety for most is often internal, as highlighted by the reasons listed above.

Signs that your teenager suffers from an anxiety disorder are as follows:

- Difficulty concentrating
- Being extremely sensitive to criticism or highly self-conscious
- Avoiding new or difficult situations
- Withdrawal from social events, activities, and situations
- Irritability
- Recurring and persistent worries and fears that interfere with daily life
- Constantly needing reassurance

Also included are sleep problems, substance abuse, a drop in grades, or regular refusals to go to school. Also, watch for medical complaints like chronic headaches or stomach aches. No two people experience anxiety symptoms in quite the same way, and you may find that your child has a combination of some or all of these symptoms. Some teens are particularly skillful at hiding their symptoms, which is not conducive to them getting the help they need.

Why do some teens suffer from anxiety while others do not? That is a complicated question to answer. No concrete scientific evidence points to a root cause.

Risk factors include:

- The environment the teen is currently in or grew up in, such as being exposed to toxic parents or peers
- Genetics
- Practicing potentially harmful or dangerous avoidant behaviors like drug abuse
- Experiencing any form of trauma like sexual, verbal, or physical abuse

Some medical issues can mimic anxiety. Examples include:

- Irritable bowel syndrome (IBS)
- Diabetes
- Heart disease
- Thyroid disorders, like hyperthyroidism
- Respiratory illnesses like chronic obstructive pulmonary disease (COPD) and asthma
- Use of or withdrawal from drugs or alcohol

Teens experience a unique view of the world. They are budding adults, yet can relate closely to childhood. The world can seem like a big, scary, and threatening place with the weight of so many expectations on their shoulders — both their own and those of others. In this day and age, social media is everywhere. It is almost impossible for them to get away from it or the lists of invisible social rules it places on them, to say nothing of how impossible it is to live up to the expectations.

Anxiety is not a one-size-fits-all condition. It can materialize as:

Generalized anxiety disorder (GAD)

GAD is excessive worry about everyday situations, events, and issues. These feelings persist for more than six months and do not lend themselves to the specific criteria for other types of anxiety disorders. Generally, sufferers don't experience panic attacks.

Social anxiety disorder

This disorder should not be confused with nervousness or shyness in social settings. Instead, it is a chronic and overwhelming fear of social situations. The sufferer is afraid of being watched or judged harshly by others. This fear can impair performance at work, school, and during everyday activities.

Obsessive-compulsive disorder (OCD)

Obsessions, compulsions, or both characterize this anxiety disorder. Obsessions describe persistent thoughts, impulses, or imaginings that enter the mind and trigger distress. The need to do these behaviors seems irresistible. Compulsions are recurrent acts or mental images that, when performed, bring relief from the anguish of obsessions. Excessive distress and angst occur if one does not give in to the urge.

Panic Disorder

The sufferer of this anxiety disorder has repeated panic attacks. Panic attacks are episodes of intense anxiety causing sudden waves of fear or panic. The sufferer feels as if there is a clear and present danger, even when safe. Some of the symptoms of a panic attack are as follows: racing heartbeat, a feeling of impending doom or death, difficulty breathing/hyperventilation, nausea, trembling, and feelings of detachment from reality.

Specific phobias

Phobias involve extreme and irrational fears and highlight overpowering, persistent, and unreasonable dread of specific situations, activities, or objects. Examples include claustrophobia (the fear of tight or enclosed spaces) and arachnophobia (the fear of spiders).

Separation anxiety disorder

Unlike typical clinginess, separation anxiety describes excessive alarm when separated from someone special, such as parents, or when taken away from a particular place or object. The anxious party will experience recurring and extreme distress by thinking about or anticipating being away from this loved one or their home.

The specifics of these anxiety disorders are described more fully in Book One of the series *Taming Teenage Anxiety with CBT and DBT*. No matter the particulars of your teen's anxiety disorder, one universal truth applies. You must seek treatment if anxiety interferes with your teen's day-to-day life. Hoping the problem will go away on its own will not work. Looking the other way causes the issue to fester and grow bigger. Be proactive and take action. The next chapter sets the stage for taking such action with ACT — a type of talk therapy that enables your teen to better deal with troubling emotions that may precede anxiety.

Chapter 2
Reaching Radical Resilience: The Transformative Power of ACT for Teens

Human beings are emotional creatures. These emotions come and go, ebbing and flowing like the tide caressing the shore. They range on the scale from mild to intense and everywhere in between. Feelings are neither good nor bad, yet they can be extremely painful and scary to experience.

We often embrace positive emotions with open arms but do not instinctively accept negative emotions often perpetrated by anxiety — fear, sadness, shame, loneliness, helplessness, etc. Our first reaction is often to push them away. To reject them, we use coping mechanisms to get rid of them. To the uninitiated in mental health treatment, this often means using potentially harmful coping techniques like drugs and alcohol abuse.

Learning to accept all emotions, those that are warm like the rays of the sun and those that pierce hard and deep like the stab of a knife, is important for emotional regulation and, thus, anxiety management. No one wants to walk around with a stab wound from their emotions, but rejecting them deepens the trauma. All emotions serve a purpose, and trying to eliminate those you don't want to feel is detrimental.

The solution is to accept your emotional experiences for what they are. This process is called emotional acceptance.

Participating in acceptance and commitment therapy (ACT therapy) is a step toward achieving emotional regulation and acceptance.

What is ACT?

ACT is a type of psychotherapy, meaning a patient talks to a psychiatrist, psychologist, or other mental health professional to treat mental health issues. These conversations center around helping the patient stay focused on the present moment to accept their thoughts and feelings as they are *now* without judgment. Dwelling on negative emotions means there is no forward movement. It is like sitting down to fixate on your terrible feelings. ACT helps the patient get up and dust themselves off so they can move toward healing.

Acceptance is not about resigning yourself to a terrible fate. You must make the distinction between acceptance and resignation. Acceptance does not mean your teen has to or will hold onto feeling pain for all time. It also does not mean the youth should deliberately push themselves to feel emotional distress. Instead, acceptance is about becoming aware of your feelings, acknowledging them as they are in the moment, *and* knowing they will not last forever. Even positive emotions like happiness do not always stay. Acceptance also means knowing change will come, and that is okay. Feelings are fleeting things that come and go, lasting for seconds, minutes, days, or even months. Your teen learns to let go of the struggle to feel better and just feels.

Pronounced like the word "act" instead of being spelled out, ACT is a behavioral therapy developed in 1986 to help mental health patients:

1. Understand what is important to them and use those values to live a more fulfilled life.
2. Learn mindfulness skills to cope with agonizing thoughts, recollections, feelings, impulses, and images so that they are less impactful on daily living.

Behavioral therapies evolved in three waves. The first wave started in the 1920s but became popular in the '50s and '60s. These therapies focused on observing behavioral changes and classic conditioning, a type of learning highlighting the relationship between a stimulus and the response to that provocation. The second wave introduced cognitive interventions in the '70s, and therapies like cognitive behavioral therapy (CBT) and rational-emotive behavior therapy (REBT) were born. REBT helps patients identify unreasonable ideas and the negative thought patterns that precede emotional and behavioral problems. CBT concentrates on changing a patient's behavior through changed thought patterns and feelings. CBT has emerged as a dominator in the world of psychotherapy since that time.

ACT is part of the third wave, which builds on the principles developed by the first two waves with mindfulness skills. Other types of therapies in this third wave are:

- Dialectical Behavior Therapy (DBT): a psychotherapy explicitly adapted for people who feel highly intense emotions. The techniques one learns help them accept themselves and manage their emotions to prevent them from engaging in potentially harmful behaviors.
- Mindfulness-Based Cognitive Therapy (MBCT): is aimed at helping people who are chronically depressed and unhappy. Cognitive therapy is combined with meditation and mindfulness to achieve this.
- Mindfulness-Based Stress Reduction (MBSR): was initially developed for stress management. This therapy also treats

disorders like anxiety and depression with intense mindfulness training.

When there are so many types of psychotherapies to choose from, how can you be sure that ACT is the right one for your teen?

ACT is beneficial to treat:

- Anxiety disorders
- Regulating stress from preparing for exams in addition to overall stress regulation
- Depression
- Phobias
- Substance abuse
- Eating disorders
- Psychosis
- Obsessive-compulsive disorder (OCD)

We call the first wave of behavioral therapies classical behaviorism because the only focus is on human behavior. The second wave added cognition to the equation so that the formula of thought and belief became intertwined with behavior. The third wave introduced mindfulness to develop greater levels of awareness.

With the third wave, variations in the therapies occur. ACT differs from MBSR and MBCT, which aim to reduce stress and increase reasoning with mindfulness. These latter therapies show significant effectiveness in treating anxiety and depression. On the other hand, people who have borderline personality disorder are more likely to benefit from participating in DBT.

ACT can help individuals like your teen, but couples and groups can take advantage of the mindfulness teachings it focuses on. A session with an ACT-certified therapist can be brief, but medium-term and long-term meetings are possible. The therapist typically creates mindfulness practices during these sessions based on what they learned during their years of qualification. These practices can be individualized and even co-created with patients. ACT therapists do not rely strictly on textbook procedures. As such, formal mindfulness meditation is only one of the many ways to develop awareness.

We live in difficult times. Added to the particular challenges teens face, it is no wonder that increased statistics indicate mental health trouble in that age group. ACT helps teens become more tolerant of difficulties encountered in all areas of life. It teaches teens to reframe negative thoughts and feelings to gain the perspective that problems only last for so long. Change always comes. With such a view, it is easier for them to confront struggles rather than hide from them. Hiding does not make anxiety symptoms go away. It only delays the inevitable. The faster they acknowledge and admit to their emotions and feel what they feel, even the hard-to-deal-with emotions, the quicker they can move on. A 2018 study highlighted that ACT has the potential to impart positive change in patients who practice the processes in the long haul.

This effectiveness, however, is comparable to other types of therapy like CBT. This fact suggests someone who finds relief using ACT may also find the same benefit in a different treatment. A few advocates for CBT have claimed that many therapies within the third wave of behavioral therapies do not present a significantly different approach compared to CBT.

The Six Core Processes of ACT for Teens

The basis of ACT is to help your teen accept their experiences daily without trying to evaluate or change them. Your teen learns to receive their thoughts and feelings as they are instead of avoiding or fighting them. Guilt is often the reason for preventing and tackling these emotions and sensations, but ACT teaches there is no need to feel guilt when we simply acknowledge and observe them.

Mindfulness is encouraged to pave the way to acceptance. The core processes that promote mindfulness in ACT are:

Acceptance

Our instinct is to avoid harmful and potentially negative experiences. After all, not many people go barreling toward pain and despair, and rightfully so. However, it is essential to fully experience life's ups and downs. Acceptance is the deliberate choice to allow hurtful experiences to exist without trying to change them into something else or denying their right to be. ACT allows for making room for painful feelings, thoughts, and urges in your teen's life. They learn to let them come and go without a fight because they only get bruised and banged up in the process.

Cognitive defusion

Defusion separates an emotion or triggering stimulus from a behavior or unwanted emotion. The norm is to go through this cycle:

thought-emotion-action

Defusion breaks this cycle to give more control. The ACT patient learns to develop a rapport with their thoughts and feelings instead of falling back on avoidant behavior. ACT encourages patients to face displeasing thoughts, feelings, and experiences head-on. Often, things seem big and scary when we hide from them. They take up more space in our minds. Exposure reduces them down to size. They become more manageable and have less power over how we act and react.

Being present

The world is massive and scary. However, it has countless wonders and beautiful things to see, feel, and experience. The only way to experience one aspect is to embrace the other. ACT encourages an attitude of curiosity and openness so that your teen can fully engage with the here and now. The past is gone, and the future may never come. The only time in which we can genuinely engage is the present.

Self as context

We are not our thoughts and feelings. Instead, our consciousness experiences this content. As such, thoughts and feelings do not affect the core of who we are. Thoughts and feelings change and continue to evolve with time. But no matter how you view yourself currently or how you think or feel, you will not change. You will remain you.

Values

They give meaning to our lives. You must distinguish them from goals. You can accomplish goals but not values. Instead, values provide us with direction. Think of them like a compass. ACT helps your teen define what their values are. Solidifying them helps resist the temptation to fall back into past harmful thoughts and behavioral patterns.

Committed action

The best intentions are nothing without action. This ACT process enables your teen to commit to the direction consistent with their values to achieve their goals. There will be obstacles and setbacks, but the skill activates their power of resilience so they can stay strong no matter what life (and anxiety) throws at them.

How to Get Started

Several options exist when seeking a mental health professional who offers ACT. This list includes mental health counselors, psychologists, social workers, and psychiatrists. If you are already getting guidance from a mental health professional, inquire if this person has a background or experience in ACT. The Association for Contextual Behavioral Science (ACBS) and the Association for Behavioral and

Cognitive Therapies (ABCT) are valuable resources for locating an ACT-certified practitioner. ACBS is also a resource for ACT practices through audio clips, mindfulness practices, and videos. Follow the link to find an ACT practitioner: https://contextualscience.org/civicrm/profile?gid=17&reset=1&force=1

An ACT therapist needs to have the following skills:

- Be empathetic
- A good listener
- An active guide

They must guide your teen to explore themselves in a more profound, non-judgmental way that encourages awareness. The first few ACT sessions aim to build a rapport with the therapist so they can identify the patient's struggles. The therapist helps your teen identify negative thoughts, feelings, and painful memories. This action paves the road for making peace with the things your teen cannot change. Deeper awareness and identification of core values give your teen the framework to understand better what they want their life to look like. That vision may include socializing without crippling anxiety ruining the moment. That may be participating in group activities at school with anticipation and joy, not dread. It may be participating in a new hobby or sport without worrying about the perception of others watching. The vision is unique to your child.

These sessions with the therapist are hands-on and include components of mindfulness training and psychological practices. Your teen is encouraged to be active and will be given homework after each session. Doing this homework is integral to learning new coping skills and improving your teen's psychological flexibility.

Psychological flexibility describes how well a person copes with changes in life and circumstances with problem-solving and creative skills. A person with good psychological flexibility can:

- Adapt to changing circumstances
- Reshape their thought patterns and processes
- Shift their perspective
- Balance competing desires, needs, and wants in different areas of life

One of the most substantial benefits of ACT is the development of psychological flexibility. This mental flexibility lets you open your arms to thoughts and feelings when they benefit you and set them down if they do not. You can mindfully respond to your thoughts and feelings and avoid acting out impulsively for short-term gratification. Psychological flexibility allows patients to accept anxiety symptoms yet still function so that these symptoms do not have as significant an impact on their daily lives.

Many people struggle because they lack forward momentum. That is a by-product of not knowing what your goals and values are. Identification of those two is an aspect of ACT.

Many negative connotations are attached to therapy. Often, people start to improve their mental health but don't return because they doubt the therapy's effectiveness. They fail to realize that therapy is not a magic cure. Its efficacy is reliant mainly on three things:

- The relationship between the therapist and patient
- Choosing the correct type of therapy
- The patient's willingness to wholeheartedly participate in therapy

You have to shop around for the right therapist. You may have to try different personalities until you find the one that aligns with your teen's temperament. That chemistry is necessary for your teen to open up to the process.

In the world of talk therapy, several options, or flavors, if you will, exist. Not every type will suit every palate. There is evidence for psychodynamic treatment for panic disorders. Interpersonal therapy, internal family systems, and eye movement desensitization and reprocessing (EMDR) benefit certain people. If treatment aims to improve your teen's relationships with others, consider trying family therapy instead of purely individual treatment.

Do not be surprised if your teen is resistant to therapy. I urge you to be patient with your child and give a gentle nudge, so they attend at least a few weeks of treatment before calling it quits. The effectiveness of the therapy is equal to zero if your teen is not willing to put in some elbow grease to better their mental health. The therapist cannot do the work for you or your teen. Commitment to hard work on your teen's part is needed. The same goes for you being willing to provide a healthy amount of support. Changes will not happen overnight, but sticking to the program and using a therapy aligned with alleviating your teen's particular symptoms allows for gradual positive changes that lessen the pain of anxiety and lead to a better life. It is important to remember the concept when one asks, "How many therapists does it take to change a lightbulb?" The answer is, "Only one, but the lightbulb must want to change."

Now that we have discussed how vital therapy is for your teenager let's see this straight from a teen's perspective. I have interviewed two teenagers about their experiences with anxiety and the treatments they have undergone for this book. Parents and other teens should read these first-hand accounts and see that their experiences are shared and they are not alone. The following chapter contains my conversations with Olivia R. and Sam B., in their own words, only edited to protect anonymity.

Chapter 3
Voices of Resilience: Teenagers Speak Out on Battling Anxiety

An Interview with Olivia R.

LM: Tell me a little bit about yourself.

OR: I am 15 years old. I am considered old for my grade. I am an athletic person. I play soccer and lacrosse. I live in a big city.

LM: Do you like living in the city?

OR: I sometimes do. But, for example, I had COVID a little while ago, which was challenging because you can't even go outside. I didn't leave my room for a week. It has its positives and negatives. I have two siblings. I will only live with one now since the other one is going to college. I have a dog as well.

LM: Do you have any hobbies? Do those help you at all with your anxiety?

OR: I used to do some more than I do now. I've done art for a long time. I started doing it when I was six or seven. I started oil painting when I was 8. Even before my diagnosis, I found it helpful. Though I didn't realize I was anxious, it was cool because it would take all my focus in every way. I couldn't focus on anything else. I was wrapped up in that. It was an incredible feeling to be transported and work on something with total focus.

LM: What is school like for you? Is it a source of anxiety?

OR: I have been going to the same small school for my whole life since nursery, but it doesn't extend to high school. I've always had good grades, but it hasn't been easy. Like writing, I have never been able to get started on writing projects. Procrastination is probably one of my best skills. Even when it was productive procrastination, getting started was the most challenging part for me. I would ask my mom about when I was younger, like in first grade, and I would say I can't do this assignment, and she thought I was being stubborn, but I couldn't get started. I have now been diagnosed with some learning disorders that I believe cause anxiety, but also have benefits. Schoolwork is an obligation in a way, but it gets me out of bed. I have to put one foot in front of the other. I probably wouldn't get out of bed most days if I had nothing to do.

LM: What are your official diagnosis/diagnoses? Do you have any other coexisting diagnoses like depression? Do you have any physical symptoms like migraines, stomach issues, etc.?

OR: I have been diagnosed with anxiety, depression, and OCD. I have some different learning disorders, as well. I have ADHD, but not the hyperactive part. I have some learning issues tied to anxiety. I get extra time in school, which is definitely helpful. When you aren't told that you have a learning disorder, you think everyone has it easy, and you're just bad at figuring it out, which is tough.

LM: Does anyone in your family or life (relatives or friends) suffer from anxiety?

OR: My dad's side of the family is complicated, but there are definitely mental health issues. I know my grandpa suffers from anxiety and depression. I don't talk to him much about it, but my mom told me it was tough on that side of the family.

LM: When you first started to experience anxiety, do you remember where you were, what age you were, what you were doing, and what were your first symptoms? How did your symptoms evolve?

OR: I don't necessarily know when it started. But I think we found out during the summer after 5th grade, when I was doing camp, I started having many issues with my knee and walking. After a lot of testing, it turned out that I had Lyme disease in my knee, which was really rough. That situation caused me a lot of stress, and I was stuck at home because I couldn't move around enough to do camp. I've never been good at swallowing pills and was on a lot of medicine. Sometimes I don't eat enough. I was throwing up because I was taking a lot of liquid medication. I couldn't do my summer work. So, my mom wanted a neuropsychological evaluation because she felt something was off, especially because I could not do my work, and I was freaking out over it. Then, it turned out that I have executive function disorder and anxiety. We got a psychiatrist, who put me on medicine for my learning disorders instead of treating my anxiety. This mistreatment occurred because most doctors treat ADHD rather than anxiety in kids my age. When things got worse with school and other things and I was freaking out more often, she would just increase my dose. Ultimately, it became a psych alert that stressed me out more because I was on edge and wasn't eating as much. Then I started taking medicine for anxiety, which started working a lot better. But it was really tough to find the balance. I had to learn to take pills, and I didn't want to do therapy at first. It was a long walk after school. I felt like going to it, and doing it almost made me more anxious because there was no time left to do homework. I felt like everything was moving too fast. Walking all the way down and sitting there as they asked me these questions that I felt were stupid felt like a waste of my time, and it wasn't helping anything, and I should've just kept trying to muddle through how I had been. I felt this way because I didn't exactly know when I started having anxiety and because it felt like it was normal. Then, work at school became harder and harder for me to manage. I was still saying I don't need this, this isn't helping, and I would stop. Then I'd have some sort of breakdown or overwhelming event, and because I didn't want to create stress for me or anyone else so I just pushed it down until some small thing happened, and I just kind of exploded. It was tough for my siblings. They thought I was overreacting or being dramatic about things when it was my anxiety at play.

LM: What treatments and therapies have you had for anxiety specifically? You have done medication and therapy. Do you know if you have done CBT, DBT, or ACT?

OR: I have done both CBT and DBT and also outpatient therapy.

LM: Which would you say was the most helpful?

OR: It might have just been timing because I was in a rough place, and my parents didn't know what to do. I was using unhealthy coping methods, and they wanted to send me to inpatient treatment, but because of Covid, they couldn't. So I did a sort of zoom-type therapy for 9 hours a day. I couldn't do the camps that I usually did. I couldn't hang out with friends. It was from 7 am-3 pm. It wasn't fun, and I was initially against it, but in the long run, it was very helpful. If I had had regular therapy, I would have just continued to convince them and myself that I was okay and kept things the same. This way, I couldn't avoid change. It was the biggest and most effective thing that helped. I saw people who were worse off than I was situation-wise in my group, and that gave me perspective. The therapist didn't treat me like a kid. In the past, I had tried to get out of therapy because I never felt like I was getting anything out of it. Then, something would happen, and I would get sent back to therapy. No one had ever sat me down and fully told me what anxiety was. Said, you have anxiety; you overthink things. I felt like I had always done that, but when I heard specifics from other group members, I realized how much I did due to anxiety. Also, when I thought things weren't working, I felt I was wasting my parents' money. But during intensive outpatient therapy, I learned a lot.

For example, I have OCD, though I didn't know that until way after I was diagnosed with the other issues. Before my diagnosis, I thought maybe everyone felt and acted like maybe I was just bad at managing life. I used to think OCD meant things being neat and organized, and here I am, flipping a shoe 15 times or else everyone I love will die. So, I learned OCD is different than what I had heard, especially since my room is a mess! I realized my OCD gets worse when my anxiety is terrible, so if I focus on my anxiety, the OCD gets better. I also realized it wasn't my parents saying they didn't want to deal with me. They didn't know how. I didn't know how. So they got me someone who did know how.

LM: What treatment are you undergoing right now?

OR: I call my therapist every other week. I used to go in person, and that sucked for me. I felt like I couldn't talk to someone face-to-face about these issues. I used to do Zooms when Covid happened. It was okay, but it kind of stressed me out. I have always had problems with my self-image. It was also hard to take myself seriously when I was looking at myself in a box on the screen. I'm trying to talk about my anxiety; meanwhile, I have a million thoughts while staring at myself. I found out over time that the option that works best for me is talking to my therapist over the phone because I can be in a comfortable space and more relaxed. I can also speak without having to see myself.

LM: Tell me a moment when you remember feeling the most anxiety. What were the circumstances, and how did you handle them?

OR: After finishing treatment, I was doing okay for a little while. Then my dog, who is my best friend in the world, became ill. He is seven and typically very active. He became very lethargic and began vomiting, and we didn't know the cause. We took him to the vet, and they didn't know what was causing the illness. He wasn't eating and he continued to vomit. We took him to the animal ER. They hospitalized him on an IV, and he kept getting worse. They weren't sure what was wrong. They called and said if he kept going like this without improvement, he wouldn't make it through the night. A week before this, he had been totally fine. That was really tough. It was during this crisis that my OCD kicked in. I would think if I did this, everything would be ok and he would recover. My anxiety was horrible during this time as well. I couldn't go to school or see friends. I shut down completely. I wouldn't talk to anyone. I would snap at people. My friends thought I was ghosting them. Afterward, I realized I didn't handle it well at all, and now I know what to do better in the future. I have my therapist's number. I call her when I am stressed out or anxious. She helped me during that time to realize it wasn't helping me to stay at the hospital and to go home and get some rest.

LM: Have you ever done mindfulness meditation, or are there other coping skills that you use that have helped?

OR: I have trouble sleeping, so I have used meditations to help me sleep. I practice progressive muscle relaxation and use self-massage because my muscles can get really tight. My back and neck still do get very tense. I've had organizational people come to help me get organized, which helps my anxiety. Someone came to the house to help me learn how to meditate. One thing I have learned is that one thing links to the next thing. If I stress about a bunch of things, if I focus on one thing, like getting more sleep, it helps all of it. When my anxiety is down, my OCD is down, and everything becomes more manageable. I have found sleep to be challenging but really important. I have gotten better at figuring out healthy coping mechanisms that work for me. I have learned a lot of coping skills. But a lot of them don't work for me. Maybe they work for some people, but not for me. I find it essential to have at least a handful of things that work for you. One of the good things I always do when I am super stressed is to put on a comfort show and sit with my dog. I usually watch a comfort show from when I was younger that reminds me of when life was simpler. Sometimes, there isn't an immediate solution to the problem at hand, but I am always searching for one. I can't sleep or function because I am trying to anticipate every possible way a situation can go when, in reality, I just need to take a break from ruminating on the problem. So I find this is a way to do that. It is a distraction but not an avoidance. After a good night's sleep, you can deal with the problem the next day.

LM: Do you have any apps or websites that you use for meditation or coping skills?

OR: Yes. Sometimes, I find meditations on Spotify that I play at night. I have voice memos of guided meditations on my phone. The guided meditations help keep me focused. Also, the background noise of the meditation helps me sleep because when everything is quiet, my head is louder. When I have nothing to think about, I think about everything.

LM: I used to be that way. Focusing on my breathing can help me drift off when my brain is in overdrive. But sometimes, I still need the background noise as well. Have you ever heard of the Calm app?

OR: Yeah.

LM: In the sleep section, they have this deep sleep release that I love for helping you relax before sleep.

OR: Yeah, I have Calm and sometimes do the sleep stories.

LM: I used to do those, as well.

OR: I have done Headspace for meditation as well.

LM: I have also done Headspace in the past as well.

LM: What kinds of social media do you have? Does it make your anxiety worse, neutral, or does it help your anxiety?

OR: I have Instagram, Snapchat, and TikTok. When I am really stressed out, I will go on IG, and the reels will be baby animals, which relieves stress. On TikTok, I have two accounts, one of which I don't post on. That way, I am not following any of my friends. When I am stressed out, I go on that account and see random funny videos. On the one where I follow everyone, I will see my friends doing something together and happy, and I'm not, which puts me in a worse mood.

LM: That would help many teenagers to have a separate account where they do not follow their friends, so if they want to avoid FOMO (Fear of Missing Out), they can do that.

LM: Looking back, do you have any regrets? Maybe something anxiety caused you to do? A therapy you wish you had tried sooner?

OR: Yeah. I ultimately learned from my regretful activities. Self-harm was something I struggled with for a while and something I regret doing. Also, I was self-medicating with marijuana for a bit. I was not hanging out with the best people at one point, and I thought it would help my anxiety. In the end, it didn't help, and it was one of the reasons I ended up in outpatient therapy. Although I didn't want to do outpatient therapy, I learned a lot from it. Obviously, I have a lot of regrets.

LM: How are you doing now in terms of your anxiety? On a scale of 1-10? Ten is the worst, non-functional, needing hospitalization, and one is entirely free from anxiety. Also, how are your relationships with your family and friends or romantic partners now?

OR: I am at a point where I realize that I don't think I will ever be without anxiety at any point in my life. It is not something that just goes away. I will be managing this forever. But if I look back to this time last year, it helps because I see how far I have come, especially when I feel like I can't keep going. Instead of spending nine hours a day in therapy this summer, I am spending nine hours a day as a camp counselor. I talk to my therapist every other week, and I am fully open and honest. Before, I questioned the usefulness of therapy and would try to convince them I was okay. Obviously, it changes by the day, but on a scale from 1-10 of what I can handle, I would say a good 7. There is always room for improvement. I am personally really proud of how far I have come. I have a boyfriend and friends I can talk to when I am upset instead of shutting down. I have people other than my therapist. I have found that I can have friends and a relationship without wholly relying on someone.

LM: I think that's wonderful. I am very happy for you.

Could you name the significant lessons you have learned from anxiety and your treatment?

OR: There isn't just one solution. No therapy works for everyone. It isn't one size fits all. I know most illnesses have a cure, but I have learned that anxiety is more of a condition and will always need management. Over time, you will get better at treating it and managing symptoms. It never completely goes away. Also, more people have anxiety than you think. I think some people are undiagnosed because they don't have the resources. When I went to outpatient, it was helpful for me to realize there are people out there who have turned their anxiety into something good, something that motivates them to do something good in the world. It was also helpful to know I wasn't alone. I wasn't the only one who felt like I did. It was very validating. Sometimes when people say, "You're not alone," it can feel invalidating, but to meet people who have learned how to manage their anxiety was validating.

LM: What would you tell other teens with anxiety disorders about your experiences, and what lies after you get a handle on managing your anxiety? What do you want adults, family members, friends, etc., to know about anxiety?

OR: Your parents and other people can try to help you, but you have to be willing and want to get better. It does get better; everyone hears that, so it sounds cliché. But you do have some control over the situation. When I was doing outpatient therapy, it was really tough because I felt like my parents were telling me, "You're doing this," and I felt like it wasn't for me. It was just something I was being forced to do. And it meant I couldn't do the things I wanted to do that summer. But towards the end of it, my mom saw me getting a lot better. She allowed me to go to soccer camp at the end of summer, which felt like a reward for all my hard work, and I was happy. I didn't need to convince my parents anymore that I was ok to prevent people from getting stressed. I had fun at camp and was so happy.

LM: That is all the questions I have. Thank you so much!

OR: When you sent out the request for teens to interview and had the word overcome in there, I was concerned because I know I have been successful at managing my anxiety, but I wouldn't say I have overcome my anxiety. But I hope what I have said will be helpful for the book and other teens.

LM: What you said will be very helpful to other teens. Thank you!

An Interview with Sam B.

LM: Can you tell me a little bit about yourself? Your age, family members, pets, etc.

SB: My name is Sam. I use they/them pronouns. I live with my mom. We have a dog and a cat. I am 18 and a senior in high school.

LM: Do you have any hobbies, and do any of them help with your anxiety?

SB: I enjoy art, which may be what I want to pursue as a career. My art helps a lot with my anxiety. I also use it to indicate when my anxiety is getting worse. Recently, I became very burnt out and my therapist and mom discovered that I hadn't drawn in two weeks, which is a very long time for me.

LM: Does your art change based on how you feel, anxiety-wise?

SB: Probably. It is not something I notice as much. My art is something that goes with the flow.

LM: What is going to school like for you? Is it a source of anxiety?

SB: Yes. School is probably one of the biggest sources of anxiety for me. It causes more anxiety than work does for me. I think it is because I know everybody at school vs. at work. At work, it is mostly random strangers. It's been a lot better this year, though. So that's good.

LM: What specifically about school causes anxiety? Is it issues with friends or academics?

SB: Some of it is how others perceive me. That has always caused me to have anxious thoughts. It was to a point where I would purposely not wear certain things because I was worried someone would make fun of me for it. But lately, I have been better at fighting back those intrusive thoughts and wearing what I like. Also, academically it used to be that if I got anything below an A, I would feel like my whole world was falling apart.

LM: Changing subjects a little...do you play sports or exercise regularly?

SB: I snowboard.

LM: That's great.

SB: But that's very seasonal. I try my best to keep up with it, but I am not sure I can do it this year. I try to exercise regularly, but it doesn't often happen.

LM: What is your official diagnosis or diagnoses? Is it generalized anxiety or OCD, etc.?

SB: A year ago, I started going to a psychiatrist. He has been helping my anxiety and seeing if I qualify as neurodivergent. He is also assisting me with my transition. I have been diagnosed with social anxiety disorder, adjustment disorder with mixed anxiety, and depression.

LM: Do you have any physical manifestations of your diagnoses? For instance, I have anxiety and suffer from migraines, fibromyalgia, and IBS.

SB: I am not sure if I have anything like that, but last year, there was a big family issue that was a significant source of anxiety. When I went to school, I developed spots on my skin because I was so anxious about the family stuff, plus school. It was so stressful. I also started having liver complications, which caused me to take medication and was quite painful.

LM: Wow, that is scary. I know that can happen, but I have never met anyone who has had that happen. Does anyone in your life, family or friends, deal with anxiety?

SB: My mother does, and I wouldn't be surprised if more people in my extended family do as well, but no one has had an official diagnosis. A lot of my friends have anxiety.

LM: How did it feel when you first started to experience anxiety? What age were you?

What were you doing? What were your first symptoms, and how have they evolved?

SB: I would guess around 4th grade. That was when I started going through puberty. It's been so long that it doesn't feel like I have ever lived without anxiety. It has been much more manageable over the past year because I started anxiety medications and went to therapy in the last couple of years. I started realizing the level of anxiety I have isn't normal. For a long time, I thought everyone had the same level of anxiety I had and that I just wasn't dealing with it well. So, finding out that my normal wasn't the stereotypical normal was a huge insight. I still have moments like that sometimes where I find out something I am experiencing, or feeling isn't necessarily typical. And it's just because I have a heightened level of anxiety.

LM: I completely understand that. The challenge is figuring out how to cope with that.

Do you remember any actions you took when you first started to experience anxiety? If so, do you remember how you managed? Or did you cope as well as you possibly could because you didn't realize it was abnormal?

SB: I remember I felt sick a lot back then. I frequently visited the school nurse. The nurse would always send me back to class because there was nothing physically wrong with me that she could tell. I remember crying because I was so anxious about getting tests and homework assignments correct. There wasn't a reason to get that upset over those things because I would have been okay no matter what happened. But my anxiety was so high that I caused my entire self to shut down and become so overwhelmed that I would start crying. It was to the point that, rarely, I would take a mental health day and not go to school. Other than that, I can't think of anything else. It was so long ago.

LM: Did your family or friends notice you suffered greatly from anxiety? Or were they clueless as to what was going on with you?

SB: I formed some friendships around that time and am still close to them today. They are also as anxiety-ridden as I am, though. There was a sense of community in that regard. Around this time I was going through puberty, so my mom thought that was the source of my anxiety. She has always been there for me and comforts me when I melt down and need extra support. She helps me study, as well.

LM: But it was only this year that you got specific therapy for anxiety, correct?

SB: Yes. We didn't realize that we lived in an abusive household until a year or two ago. So, that was part of the reason why it took so long for me to get help. My mom and I realized it was an actual issue and not something random or something caused by my being in an abusive household.

LM: Do you know what kind of specific therapies you have had from your therapist? CBT? DBT? ACT?

SB: We mainly do talk therapy. We considered doing CBT at one point but haven't done that yet.

LM: You said you are in therapy currently, and has it helped a lot?

SB: Oh yes. It is very relieving to have someone to talk to regularly. Right now, I haven't had an appointment in two weeks because I have been so busy. I get to see my therapist tomorrow, and I am excited because it has been a while. I usually meet up with him once a week.

LM: Are you seeing a psychiatrist who does therapy? Or two different people?

SB: No. I am seeing a therapist and a psychiatrist.

LM: Are there any coping skills you use, like meditation, yoga, progressive muscle relaxation...anything like that?

SB: Sometimes, I meditate when trying to fall asleep. I also listen to music a lot. It helps me cope with different situations and is an easier activity to do when you are struggling.

LM: What kind of music do you like?

SB: I like musicals and indie pop or alternative music. I'm not sure how to describe it.

LM: That's ok. I would struggle to describe my favorite genre of music as well.

LM: Can you tell me when you felt the most anxious? If you don't want to tell me the exact circumstances, you don't have to, but can you tell me how you handled it?

SB: Typically, my anxiety is always there. It is not something that leaves and then comes back in a flood. I guess one good example is when I was driving home with my mom, and we saw a cat on the side of the road. And I thought it was one of our cats, which would have been unusual as they are indoor cats. I was freaking out at the possibility that it was our cat. We don't have any outdoor cats because of where we live. It wouldn't have been the first time one of our cats escaped. Luckily, my mom was there to keep me calm and help me find the cat. When we did find the cat, we realized it was not ours. The cat was very confused about why we were so concerned about it, haha. I went home and gave my cat a lot of pets due to that situation, which helped a lot. My mom's presence helped a lot since she believed it might be our cat instead of dismissing me outright.

LM: That's great that you have such a supportive mom. Now, on to a touchy subject. In the course of your life, have you ever had thoughts of suicide?

SB: I have had passive suicidal ideation. I have never had a plan to complete suicide. The only reason I am alive is because of my friends and the thought of what my death would do to my mother. I also have thoughts of wanting to sleep forever, not to be awake anymore. So it is less of a plan, and rather that if I didn't have the people I care about in my life, I wouldn't care about dying, and maybe I would complete suicide.

LM: Have you ever performed any self-harm, like cutting or burning yourself? Or skin picking, etc.?

SB: Nothing like cutting or burning, but I have unhealthy habits like biting my lips and picking around my fingernails. I wear rings to help distract my hands. Recently, we had our fall play, and my poor lip split in the middle due to the amount of stress I was under and how much I "worried" over my lip. Now that the play is over, it is healing.

LM: Now for a lighter question: what kinds of social media do you have?

SB: I have Tumblr, which is the main one I use. I also have YouTube and TikTok. Those are the main ones I use. I also have Instagram and Snapchat, but I never use them. I also have Twitter because my friends have it, but I don't really use it.

LM: Do you think those cause anxiety or help your anxiety?

SB: It tends to be a mix of both. Tumblr and YouTube tend to be pretty personalized. I usually go there to entertain or distract myself. Typically the content is video games or music related. TikTok tends to be the main offender for worsening my mental health. But that seems to be the way it is set up as a platform. Its ForYou page is really good, but I am in the LGBT+ community, so I get a lot of that kind of news. So any bad thing that happens in the community, I find out really quickly.

LM: I hear you. I spend time on TikTok, which you may find weird for someone my age, but I get LGBT+ news because I am an ally, and this week I have been doing a lot of scrolling to protect my mental health in the wake of the shooting in Colorado. There is only so much heartache one can take. Plus, shootings cause a tremendous amount of anxiety for me. It is wise to avoid Doom Scrolling.

SB: I had to hear about it a lot because I got my name legally changed today. So it was like, yay, am I setting myself up for something like this?

LM: Other teens have told me that social media causes anxiety because they can see their friends socializing without an invite. Is that ever an issue for you?

SB: No, my friends and I struggle to get together these days because we are all so busy.

LM: That may be the age difference. The other teenagers I interviewed, plus my daughter, are younger than you and struggle with the FOMO of seeing their friends socialize without them.

LM: Looking back, do you have any regrets? Maybe something anxiety caused you to do, a therapy you wished you had tried sooner, something to that effect.

SB: I have always wished I had started therapy sooner. It was just one of those things where you look back and say if only I had recognized this three years ago, five years ago.

LM: Were you successful with your first therapist?

SB: No, actually. I started therapy right as COVID hit. My mom and I drove to the first therapy appointment, and I did not like her vibe. Her vibe was weird and off. For instance, I was discussing how I have imposter syndrome, and she had no idea what I was talking about. So I thought, I don't think this is going to work. That was a Wednesday. That Friday, our school shut down. So, now I meet with my current therapist over Zoom. I could go in person, but since my schedule is super crazy, it is easier to continue online. My general practitioner recommended this therapist to me, and we have had a good working relationship.

LM: It is so common that it is almost the norm for your first therapist not to work out. It is so important for adults and teenagers to hear that information, especially from a fellow teenager. If the first therapist does not work out, it is not a reflection on you or a reason to throw in the towel. Of course, it is frustrating to have to start over with a new person, especially if your story is fraught with trauma, but in the end, it is worth it when you find the right therapist for you.

SB: I have also had to do that with medications, and knowing that the drug wasn't right for me and that it didn't mean I wouldn't get better was important.

LM: Those are essential insights. In what ways do you think anxiety has changed your life? Do you look at your life differently now? Do you feel like a different person now that you recognize your anxiety and are working through it? Are your relationships different now in terms of family and friends?

SB: I think so. I feel like I have always had anxiety, and I will always have anxiety. The key is to bring it to a manageable level. I have seen how much I was hiding from the world and myself. My transition is closely linked to my anxiety. The fact that I got my name changed today is fantastic. The fact that I could tell my mom, tell my friends, and come out and say who I truly am is terrific. My anxiety held me back for a long time. It still does a little bit, but it is much better now. Driving is a good example. I got my permit right when I turned 16. I didn't start driving until this year at 18 years old. I was so afraid that I would hurt someone while driving that I didn't do it. It was a frequent topic during my therapy sessions. Even though I procrastinated on it, it really helped to have the resources of my therapist to get me through it. Now, while I'm driving, I don't always feel super calm, but driving can be nice. I don't feel like I am going to explode every time I step into the car.

LM: Can you name some lessons you have learned from your experiences with anxiety? For instance, I have anxiety; I am not anxiety.

SB: A big thing I learned during this is to be nicer to myself. My anxiety fueled my inner critic. I am not the best at affirmations, but when I do something stupid or wrong, my internal dialogue is a lot nicer than it used to be. It is incredible how a simple change can improve my mental state.

LM: What would you say to other teens who have anxiety disorders about your experiences of what lies after you begin to manage your anxiety successfully?

SB: I would say never stop being yourself. Anxiety is always going to be an uphill battle, no matter what. But it will get easier to manage. You will get better resources and support groups as your life goes on. And it might not always be perfect. I know I have had to scratch the book of my life when I found the groups unhelpful. But eventually, you find some sort of balance for yourself.

LM: What do you want to say to adults, family members, friends, etc., about what it is like to have anxiety? Something that would help them understand it and know how to help.

SB: The first thing I would say is don't say it will be ok, as it is not really reassuring, and it doesn't help. The thing that helps is being there for that person and being able to offer help when they need it. That doesn't mean asking if they need help every 20 minutes. You have to respect their boundaries and help within those boundaries. It will not always be easy to help or be helped. With time and effort, the person with anxiety tends to get better.

LM: Last question, open-ended. What do you think the future holds for you?

SB: Currently, I plan to go to college. We call it in our house, becoming an emancipated adult, which is very much a legal term. I would like to get a good job. I would like to find someone with whom I could spend my life. And most importantly, continue to be me. I am finally in a place where I can be myself.

LM: Is there anything else you want to add?

SB: Cats add a lot to your life if you can have them. Pets help quite a bit. They seem to know when I am upset and will sit with me. My dog will bring me all his toys.

LM: I wholeheartedly agree. My cats and dog are my furry supports that take my sorrow and give nothing but love back in return. We don't deserve them!

Thank you so much for allowing me to interview you. I think your insights will be beneficial to teenagers who have anxiety.

SB: You're very welcome.

Now that we have heard about the real-life experiences of teenagers in the 2020s, let's switch gears and discuss the event that started that decade, the COVID-19 pandemic. The pandemic hit all of us mentally time and again. But no two people or age groups were affected the same. The next chapter dives into how the pandemic affected teens specifically, and how they can cope in the aftermath.

Share Your Thoughts and Make a Difference

Helping Teens Navigate Anxiety with ACT

"The best way to find yourself is to lose yourself in the service of others."

— –Mahatma Gandhi

Are you ready to make a difference in someone's life? Imagine a world where teenagers struggling with anxiety find hope and support through your words. Together, we can unlock the power of generosity and kindness.

As you embark on this journey with us through "Taming Teenage Anxiety with ACT," I invite you to share your thoughts and experiences in a review. Your words have the potential to change lives and inspire others.

Here's why your review matters:

1. **Helping Teens:** Your review can reach a teenager battling constant worry and stress, offering them guidance and understanding.
2. **Supporting Parents:** Parents worried about their child's well-being can find solace and practical strategies through your review.
3. **Spreading Awareness:** By sharing your feedback, you contribute to raising awareness about the importance of mental health support for young individuals.

To leave a review, simply follow this link: https://www.amazon.com/review/review-your-purchases/?asin=B0D4V3QRBJ or scan the QR code below. It takes less than a minute but can make a lasting impact.

Thank you for being part of this meaningful journey. Your support means everything. Spread the love by recommending this book to someone who could benefit from it. As a token of our gratitude, we're excited to share valuable insights and strategies with you in the upcoming chapters. Together, we can make a positive impact on the world.

Warm regards,

Lillian Middleton

Chapter 4

When the World Stands Still: Navigating Teenage Anxiety Amidst the COVID-19 Pandemic

Life was imperfect, but we, as a global community, had a sense of normalcy before 2020. Then, the first official case of COVID-19 was recorded on December 31, 2019. Our understanding of normality left us as if it had never existed.

One of our standard coping mechanisms is to mentally distance ourselves from the bad things happening. Many people wanted to think that COVID-19 was happening worlds away and would never affect us and our families. We wanted to believe that we could watch the heartbreak from the comfort of our homes on our televisions and smart devices and sympathize with other people from afar. We wanted to believe we, as a Western society, would not be tremendously affected by the virus. Within a few weeks, the merit of that belief dissolved into nothing. People got sick. People died. Walls became prisons, confining people to their homes without a choice. Life turned upside down with routines disrupted, constant worry and panic, and what seemed like never-ending horrific news reports.

When I wrote this book (August 2023), the WHO had recorded over 768 million cases of COVID-19 and over 6.9 million deaths from the virus worldwide. This reality came with skyrocketing rates of mental health decline. People were rightly depressed and anxious due to an uncertain future on the horizon.

The level of devastation made this nightmare seem like it would never end, but we are reclaiming the pieces of our lives that brought comfort, security, and happiness. We no longer have to submit to a fate of sickness and death. We are fighting against this virus with treatments and vaccines that are highly effective and have high success rates. At this time, we still need to be vigilant to protect the safety of our families, friends, and ourselves. But physically, we are seeing strides toward improvement.

Mentally, it's another story.

The Census Bureau has reported a considerable increase in depression and anxiety statistics for all age groups in the United States since the onset of the pandemic. Luckily, professionals and organizations have recognized and addressed these increases nationally. They are utilizing a range of cognitive behavioral therapies to treat the psychological issues that inevitably arose from the suffering that ensued during this challenging time in history. ACT is one such therapy. Mindfulness, problem-solving therapy, and other approaches have also come in handy.

The virus stripped us of a fundamental human right: the right to choose. To choose how we spend our time. To decide where we went and with whom we interacted. It even stole our positivity to a large extent. The outlook was bleak and dark. But as we recover, we are reclaiming our power. We do have a choice in how we respond to the pandemic. This chapter in our lives may have gotten off to a rocky start, but we can still choose what words to pen moving forward.

For a teen suffering from anxiety, taking control of their thoughts and feelings might seem impossible in the wake of the pandemic. That limiting belief is understandable, though. Adolescence is supposed to be a time of exploration - of oneself and the wider world. Teens are supposed to be testing their new wings in this phase of life. Home confinement made that impossible. Trying new things, going to new places, and meeting new people was inconceivable. COVID-19 prevented teens from stretching the boundaries they knew as kids. They needed that time to make mistakes and learn life lessons. They needed that time to determine how they fit into their communities and peer groups. Their development was irrevocably interrupted.

Interpersonal interactions and relationships are fundamental for healthy developing teens. Human beings are social creatures. Hard-wired into our DNA is the need to be around and interact with others like us. So ingrained is this need that we feel a burst of pleasure – activated by the brain's reward center - when we socialize. In many ways, teens feel more rewarded than adults when this contact happens. They need to spend time with their friends. It is all part of the process of discovering who they are. It lets them gather the courage to spread their wings when it is time to leave the nest.

Other teens are not the only contact teenagers are used to. While peers of similar age and interests gave them a sense of comfort, other people outside that age bracket offered support. Apart from their parents, the support came from extended family, teachers, coaches, religious leaders, and more. We are used to hearing about the play younger kids need for their mental development, but it is often a missed point that teens also need playful recreation. They used to get that during after-school and sporting events. Schools also offer mental health services like counselors. More than 30 percent of adolescents receive mental health care from their schools. All of these caring networks were interrupted. It is crucial now more than ever for parents to be a stable support system that uplifts and empowers teens. When they do not get such contact, teens feel bored and alone. This isolation activates the opposite reaction in their brains. They feel penalized.

They have had to forfeit many milestones. Birthdays. Graduations. Religious and cultural commemorations. All of these events signify growth and development. These are rites of passage. However, since 2020, teens have not gone through these ceremonies like they used to. Either they have been altered to fit the "new normal," or they miss them entirely. To compound the traditional items that make teens anxious, they now have this sense of loss and might not even understand what it signifies. They needed these confirmations that they were crossing the threshold into adulthood.

With the odds stacked against them, how do they cope? I wrote this chapter to answer that question in detail.

Strategies to support teen coping

Therapists often say parenting is 20 percent what you teach and 80 percent who you are. Nature designed children to base their behavior on their models. They see and copy much more than you know. The best way to support your teen through pandemic anxiety is to start with yourself. Energy comprises the universe. The sun, the stars, the moon, the planet, and everything on it give off energetic forces. You, I, and everyone else also take in and give off energy. The things we think and feel turn into frequencies. Even though we can't see them, the waves radiate outward.

When we are happy, we give off specific frequencies. That is why smiles and laughter are infectious. On the opposite end of the spectrum, when we are worried, sad, or anxious, we also transfer that energy. Adults were just as affected as younger people by this pandemic. It turned our lives upside down and threw our routines out the window. We also had a hard time coping. Help your teen by first helping yourself with self-care. On planes, safety regulations always emphasize the "put your oxygen mask on first" concept. As parents, we are hardwired to leave ourselves behind and put our kids first, but the best way to do that, in this case, is to show your teen how to put in the challenging but rewarding effort of coping with stress. Take care of yourself to show your teen how to face the challenges life will inevitably throw at them.

Regulating emotions is a learned ability, not naturally ingrained. As such, children and teens have yet to develop the powers of self-control fully. They need help in the form of co-regulation from adults who can guide them through life. Through co-regulation, kids and adolescents learn to soothe and manage emotions that cause distress. They feel secure in the healthy connections they have formed with dependable adults. They watch and imitate how their caregivers and other trusted sources cope with proceeding when faced with the same or similar situations. In the same way, they do the opposite if the role model provided is frantic in their thinking and actions in times of trouble.

Acting calm and composed when confronted with chaos is not enough. Your actions need to align with your emotions. Otherwise, you will confuse the youth when your behavior and the energy you radiate contradict each other. The director of the Center for Parent and Teen Communication describes it this way:

> "Looking like a duck calmly gliding on the water is not actually the answer. While it may lend stability, it doesn't teach strategy. As parents, we want to look like the duck moving through the water but also let our children see that our feet are paddling quickly underneath to help us stay afloat."
>
> — Dr. Ken Ginsburg

Helping teenagers manage their mental health often starts with addressing the parent's mental health. As parents, we have so much to figure out: how to put food on the table, ensure we have a place where we can all lay our heads, and keep a steady income from month to month. Many parents feel they are about to crash as the mental load chases them. If you crash and burn, your child will not have the steady support they need from you. You can't create a healthy, healing environment for that child to unload their burden.

Practicing self-care is one sure way to decrease the incidence and severity of anxiety symptoms. Teach your teen these skills by providing them with a model to mimic. Safely spend time with other people who bring joy and laughter into your life. Strive to eat healthily. Indulge in a weekly exercise routine. Get the amount of shut-eye you need every night. Even if you have to use a steel blade, carve time out of your schedule to relax, even if that means sitting back and doing nothing. Try relaxing coping skills such as yoga, meditation, enjoying a hobby, or listening to music that calms you. As you loosen up, encourage your teen to de-stress in ways that make them happy. Be consistent and set up routines for these self-care activities. Highlight how important it is that they do the same. Show your teen how they can methodically take control of their minds and bodies one day at a time by doing the same thing.

You deserve to feel the delight of good mental health just as much as your teen. When your child is hurting, it can feel "selfish" to invest in self-care. Being completely selfless is not the goal of parenting. Parenting shouldn't be an endless pit of self-sacrifice and suffering. You need a strong sense of self for children to build their own.

As you integrate self-care into your household routine, you can better see the results of active steps helping your teen get a sound mental footing to push back against pandemic anxiety. Here are a few strategies at your disposal.

Develop a dialogue with your teen

Don't be surprised if your teen has clammed up as a coping mechanism to deal with all that has happened since the pandemic, even if that child used to be a Chatty Cathy. Encourage them to come out of their shell by opening the lines of communication. Ask open-ended questions even if they do not appear receptive. You might face a grumpy teen, but do not discredit their powers of observation. The gesture shows you care. Try saying, "Times have been rough, and you have been brave. I would like to know how you feel about it. What has been helping you cope? How can I help make it better?"

You don't need to have all the answers, but let your adolescent know you are ready and willing to support them. Sometimes, all the support that is required is a listening ear. I find this a critical point. My teen often wants me to listen and not "fix" anything.

Get back into the swing of things

The routine structure of our lives makes us feel secure and calm because we know what to expect. This makes our brain happy since it doesn't have to constantly figure things out on the fly. However, due to the pandemic, many of us woke up and went to bed at odd times. Regular mealtimes were replaced by snacking at any time. School schedules and talking to friends no longer carried familiarity.

Even now, some people have not regained a sense of normalcy. However, it's possible to re-establish that feeling of repose and certainty by implementing systems and procedures. We can resume regular times for waking up and going to bed, set times for getting dressed and eating meals throughout the day, and even schedule time away from screens.

Digital devices have paved the path to accessing social media, which can often amplify the negative feelings dredged up by the pandemic.

We will discuss social media in the next chapter.

Define the mood for moving forward

We have been stripped of the ability to plan for the future for months and years. Achieving goals and pursuing dreams are part of human nature. It caused much worry and sadness when we had to put these on the back burner to ensure our survival. We need to recapture what makes us human and change this moving forward. It is up to us parents to set the tone for an attitude of future orientation and helpfulness. This does not mean sticking your head in the sand about existing problems. We still face challenging times, but humans have always shown their greatest strength in times of adversity. We are problem-solvers. We are creative. We are resilient. Harness these powers by developing a positive mindset. It will take a lot of work, but the key is to focus on what you can control. Hold onto your teen's vision of having a better future because of your efforts now. Your actions and reactions now make a difference in the future. Show your teen this; they will copy your fortitude to fight anxiety.

Bring joy back into your life

We have lost a lot since 2020. Lives. Time. Health. Normalcy. As the number of COVID-19 infections and variants waxes and wanes, it is time to embrace finding joy in our lives again. We were living in a state of survival, and there was no room for celebration when we were concentrating on staying alive. Allow yourself to live for fulfillment again. Embrace delight and laughter even in the little things. Joy is an underrated emotion that can shine a light through the darkest times. Joy helps you make it through hard times. Connecting and being together brings us joy. Depending on infection rates, families can move celebrations outdoors or make it possible for high-risk family members to attend virtually. There is always the option of having guests wear a mask or do a rapid test before coming to an event. Then, everyone can feel a level of safety in attending.

Get help

Sometimes, despite our best efforts, we just don't have the training or tools to help our teens escape the traps in their minds. Don't give up. Don't despair. Instead, do the right thing: seek help - not just for your teen, but for yourself. There is no shame in admitting that the burden is too much for you to carry alone. It takes great courage to acknowledge that you don't know everything and need support. Getting help for yourself is a powerful statement. It says, "I deserve better than to feel this way, and so I am taking the steps to get what I am worthy of." You are providing a great role model for your teen.

Redefining Normal

It has kept many parents up at night wondering what will happen to the teens who have lived through such a dark time in human history. This group of youngsters has lost so much. We would all like to believe that, any day now, their resilience and willpower will allow them to recapture what normal used to be.

But that type of thinking is a trap. There is no going back to how it used to be. There is only moving forward and redefining what normal is. We parents need to be proactive and intentional as we develop the support systems teens need to manage the stress and anxiety this space in time has created. Every generation is shaped differently because they are exposed to different events. The pandemic has shaped this set of teens in a way that can't be undone, but there is a silver lining. We have developed a sense of community and togetherness to demonstrate our strength as a species. That strength is instilled in these teens just as much as the notion that humans need each other in many ways. That has been clearer now more than ever. These teens will make it out on the other side of this tougher and better together.

Critical Steps to Coping with the Pandemic

What does a new normal look like? How can we help ourselves and our teens adjust to life after so much has been unsettled? This section gives you the tools you need to do just that.

Normalize feelings of anxiety

The core of humanity was shaken by one of the biggest disasters we have ever faced in the last century. Feeling anxious, sad, worried, hopeless, and a host of other unrelenting emotions on the spectrum is typical. Validate your feelings and those of your teen just as you would in the wake of any frightening event. Sometimes, we are disoriented as if waking from a bad dream. Sometimes, it feels like we can't wake up from the nightmare, yet the reality is quite vivid and daunting. Being anxious at this time makes sense. After all, anxiety exists as a defense mechanism to keep us safe. Make it okay to feel what needs to be felt and acknowledged during this time. Acceptance is part of the process of moving on. It allows us to see we have a choice in how we react from here on out.

Continue being safe

Maintaining good physical health continues to be a top priority. Cases of infection from COVID-19 are fluctuating around the globe, but we shouldn't let our guard down. Do what needs to be done to start living life as freely as you can, but still, be mindful of the regulations the Centers for Disease Control (CDC) and your local health departments have put in place to protect us all. Wearing masks. Social distancing. Maintaining proper hygiene. These recommendations and more were implemented to reduce the chances of catching and spreading COVID-19. Know the importance of vaccinations and boosters; unless your doctor recommends otherwise, get them as advised. While these behaviors might be inconvenient or uncomfortable, they keep us and our families safe.

Know when worry serves a good purpose

Hundreds of millions of people have been infected with COVID-19 since it emerged, and millions have died because of it. However, billions of people inhabit this planet, so the probability of any one person catching the virus and dying from it is relatively low. While you can die from catching COVID-19, the likelihood of this becoming a fatal case is very low, especially if you are vaccinated and have received the appropriate boosters. I am by no means insinuating you ignore prevention guidelines. I am encouraging the opposite. Following these recommendations lowers the probability even more. Most people who die from the virus fall into high-risk groups, like people who have co-existing medical conditions like diabetes, obesity, and cancer, as well as people 70 years old and over. Such people must take special precautions to avoid infection.

While the presence of COVID-19 does cause us to worry, there is a productive way to enable this emotion. Worrying about getting infected, whether your livelihood will be affected by the virus, or whether the virus will ever be eradicated are all unproductive worries. They do not help you, they do not change the situation, and they only cause anxiety symptoms to pop up.

But productive worry allows you to prepare better and protect yourself and others. It leads to progress through action planning, so you are better off than you previously were. You note a problem and solve it. For example, worrying about having enough food at home to last the next few days allows you to stock up your pantry adequately in case further lockdowns occur. Another productive worry may be wondering if the people around you are wearing their masks properly. In such a case, you can gently suggest a person not following this guideline do so accordingly.

Worrying is natural, but unfortunately, you can't always steer your thoughts down a productive path. Sometimes, it will leave your control and take the unproductive path. What do you do then?

The most important thing to remember is that you can choose how you react to such thoughts. You can go down the path of least resistance and let these unproductive negative thoughts repeat themselves in an endless cycle. This leads to greater levels of anxiety and depression.

The other choice is to accept that these negative thoughts exist. Acceptance leads to embracing uncertainty and the fact that there are some things you simply cannot control. Anxiety makes it seem like only adverse outcomes are possible if things are uncertain, but uncertainty does not equal dire consequences.

A general feeling of a lack of control highlights the pandemic. This lack of control causes extreme anxiety for those prone to it. However, there was uncertainty before the pandemic. We simply accepted these unknowns as part of our day-to-day doings. Ordering food. Choosing to do something outside of what you are used to. Starting a conversation even with someone you know. Traveling by boat, car, plane, and even by foot. These activities and more have outcomes that we can never know for sure. The result can be unfortunate, but it can also be good. Acceptance of these unknowns gets you out of the paralysis of anxiety. It pushes you to take action instead. It also leads to focusing on areas you can control, such as how you react, rather than the things that are out of your hands.

Another technique for dealing with unproductive worry is to schedule a specific time in the day for worrying. Aptly call it what it is - *Worry Time*. The premise is simple. To the best of your ability, place your worries on hold until you reach the specific time of day. Dodging the intrusive thoughts until then lets you be productive during the day. Even though you might not be able to push all these thoughts to the side until *Worry Time*, some success is better than being bogged down all day by the thoughts. Often, I find by the time I get to this scheduled period, these thoughts are no longer as looming or pressing as they seemed before. Anxiety thoughts are only as threatening as the time and energy you feed into them.

Connect safely

You and your teen need to connect with other people. They bring us joy and hope, things desperately needed when anxiety rears its head. No matter the level of local positivity rates or the contagiousness of the latest variant, there are ways to connect with our friends, family, and other loved ones so we don't become isolated. The obvious and safest method is to go completely virtual. You can digitally connect with groups for yoga, meditation, exercise, practicing religion, and more. Online learning also offers opportunities for learning new skills, like mastering a musical instrument and learning new languages. How this connection happens is up to you. Compared to just a few years ago, so many choices are on the table. As the levels of contagion decrease and as weather permits, you can host gatherings and events outdoors or on a screened porch, ideally with a two-way cross breeze.

Be proactive

Inaction is just as dangerous as isolation to the mind. It is a typical precursor to depression and anxiety. Not engaging in meaningful activities stunts the growth of the mind. Make space for daily activities that add value to your and your teen's life. This value varies from person to person, but standard practices include learning new skills, connecting with others, practicing mindfulness, and practicing religion. Simply ensure these activities mean something to you. Perhaps they will educate you. Maybe they will entertain you. Some ensure frequent human connection. Whatever that value is, their presence means you look forward to them and want to do them. This way, they reduce worry and stress so you overcome feelings of helplessness and hopelessness.

Feel hopeful again

With hundreds of our days controlled by the pandemic, it can seem like the cloud of misery will never go away. This sense of hopelessness creates a general shadow over everything, but focusing on specific activities and events instead of this global outlook will rack up optimism points.

Hopelessness and helplessness often go hand in hand, like the couple in a toxic marriage. We feel helpless when we think that no matter what we do, a negative outcome is inevitable. However, this feeling of vulnerability generally comes when we focus on things we have no control over. Remove the veil of powerlessness by shifting your focus to the more minor things you do have control over. Such as organizing events that let you connect with the people you love, exercising to feel rejuvenated, learning something new as a mental exercise, and practicing mindfulness meditation to focus on the present moment rather than ruminating on the past or future. Schedule activities that help you feel more in control of the minutes throughout your day.

Focus on staying present to overcome hopelessness. The past is already gone and can't be undone. The future has not yet arrived, and we cannot dictate what will come. The present is the only time we are guaranteed. It is the only time that can bring us true joy. Defuse hopelessness by bringing yourself to the here and now when you notice a move away from that time. Objectively examine your internal world to see when feelings are masquerading as facts. Let's be clear: mine, yours, and your teen's feelings are all real. However, they are not reality. You are not the things you feel. Emotions can be so strong we mistake them for reality. Make it a habit of questioning whether this is a feeling or a fact. The more you note your feelings, the more you see that current emotions will pass. No emotion lasts forever, even though powerful emotions can seem to have taken up permanent residence. Help yourself see that negative and positive emotions are fleeting by rating their intensity as you note their presence from hour to hour. You will see that emotions change depending on several factors, like the time of day, what you're doing, and who you're interacting with. Hopelessness can make it seem like things will never be different than they are in the moment. But how can that be true if you have indisputable truth stating otherwise?

Lessen financial insecurity

The pandemic brought about a global economic recession, and many people lost their jobs and financial security. The psychological cost has been immense, as unemployment often leads to depression and anxiety. Just as you are worried about the pandemic's impact on your family's finances, it is most likely your teenager is, too. They might fear whether you will keep your job or business afloat. They might be nervous about whether the roof will remain over their heads in the coming days. They might be worried about how food will be placed on the table. It is up to you to show them that while some things cannot be controlled in this aspect of life, others can be manipulated. Just like feelings, employment and finances are subject to change.

One factor within your control is budgeting. Create a financial plan for spending and bringing in income as we transition from pandemic to endemic COVID-19. Teach your teen to do this, too, with an allowance or income from a part-time job. Find ways to enjoy life even when finances are limited. For example, if you are used to eating out frequently and have had to cut back, make mealtime at home fun. Ideas for doing so include eliciting the participation of all family members, having themed days like Taco Tuesdays, and changing locations like having blanket meals at the beach or park. Having to scale back when dollars are not as free-flowing does not have to mean a life of deprivation. Financial loss does not mean defeat. Show your teen that life can be enjoyable on a budget. Also, show them how to recover by developing systems and procedures to get back on their feet when times permit.

Help someone in need

It is rewarding to help other people. Extending that helping hand also takes the focus off helpless, hopeless, and depressing feelings. It is difficult for these feelings to take root as you do something meaningful for another person. If you know someone who is struggling, offer support as you can. Brighten someone's day by checking in to show they are in your thoughts. Your family can provide a meal for an elderly or needy person in the neighborhood. You can offer to drive someone to a destination close to your own.

Times are challenging, but this is an opportunity to show gratitude and lift spirits. Some people are often selfless in their actions, like those providing additional emotional support to your teen. Examples include camp counselors, teachers, and club leaders. Get in touch, express your appreciation for all they do, and befriend them as they allow. The more you see the impact of your presence in other people's lives, the less helpless you feel. You are making a difference. Encourage your teen to do the same so they shrug off the coat of hopelessness the pandemic has clothed us in.

Overcoming pandemic anxiety is all about taking it one step at a time. That process is getting easier to see through since we are reinventing what our new normal means. But how do we deal with a worry-inducing factor that has been with us before the pandemic and will surely outlive the virus? How do we stop our teens from being the victims of the anxiety-causing effects of social media? The next chapter delves into answering that question.

Chapter 5
The Social Dilemma: Establishing Social Media's Impact on Teenage Anxiety

Like the climbing and all-consuming crest of a tsunami, we adults have felt helpless watching the frightening rising tide of teenage anxiety statistics. Just like the devastating natural disaster, there is cause and effect. Something triggered this escalation. As we look for the instigator, it is hard not to notice the cord that has linked so much suffering through this epidemic. It is a commonality that past generations did not encounter. We see it in malls and schools. It is there on playgrounds and parks. Public transportation and our vehicles also contain this element. Not even our homes are exempt from this factor.

It feels like an ominous presence, but it is small and unassuming. Most of us (adults included) say we don't know how to survive daily without it. There is a smartphone in the hands of almost every teen in virtually every corner of this planet. A Pew Research Center survey conducted in 2018 revealed that 95 percent of US teens (ages 13 to 17 years) have access to a smartphone. Forty-five percent of those teens are accessing the internet on a near-constant basis on their devices. But what exactly are they connecting to online with such unremitting resolve?

These devices are brought to life by social media notifications time after time. Instagram. TikTok. Snapchat. YouTube. These and so many other social media platforms are holding teens' attention for an average of seven and a half hours of screen time daily. This figure does not include time spent doing schoolwork.

Teens are consuming content in mere blinks of their eyes. Videos. Pictures. Memes. Most importantly, they are exchanging information and communicating in many forms. They are mesmerized by what happens on the instrument that seems permanently attached to their palms. This enthrallment frustrates many parents. We want alone time with our teens. We want genuine connections when we are together with them. But the device often holds their attention, leading to distracted answers, mumbled responses, and a wall of silence. Is it any wonder we often want to pull the device out of our ward's hand and chuck it out a window?

We might have good reason to feel this way since the release of the first iPhone in 2007 coincides with a rise in teenage sleeplessness, worry, loneliness, and substance use disorder. A study by the *Association of Psychological Science* found that 33 percent of teens who spent two hours daily on a smart device became a suicide risk. This percentage increased to 48 percent in teens who spend five hours a day on such a device. It doesn't help the cause of communication and interaction via smart devices and digital technology when we see teens reduced to tears because of social media usage.

No matter how much we wish our teens would put their phones down so they can connect with us more, can we undoubtedly say social media and the prevalence of digital interactions are causes of teenage anxiety?

The answer cannot be nailed down to a solid yes or no answer. Instead, more precisely, the answer is complicated. Psychiatrists are prone to calling social media an anxiety accelerant rather than the cause of it. The correlation between teen anxiety and social media does not equate to causation.

Social media is evolving far too quickly for us to pick apart just how it impacts the mental health of teens and other users. This makes the results of many studies inconclusive and inconsistent. Undoubtedly, social media enables social comparisons – a state that will ultimately lead to anxious thoughts.

Social comparison is comparing things about us (like our opinions, behaviors, social status, abilities, and successes) to other people to better assess ourselves in those areas. Teens are using social media to determine their personal and social worth based on how they compare to others they see on these platforms.

We tend to make downward social comparisons to people we think are less attractive than us, have less worldly possessions, or are less skilled in a particular area. Self-esteem can rise because we believe we are in a better position than others.

But we live in an age where these social media platforms come with filters and other tools that allow users to showcase themselves in the best light - sometimes in an untrue or unrealistic light. Most people will not post their faults or things they perceive as flaws on social media. They want others to believe they are living their best life by driving fast cars, living in huge mansions, eating in 5-star restaurants for breakfast, lunch, and dinner, and succeeding in every endeavor they pursue. These are standards and expectations created on these same platforms. Often, what is posted on social media is a skewed view of reality. That is the image portrayed to teens. Those expectations are not what most people can live up to, and most teens are making upward social comparisons. Their self-esteem is reduced, and they think that these people on social media are 'better' than them.

Likes, follows, and the number of 'friends' teens have on these platforms are feeding them data about what other people think of them, their appearance, and their opinions. When they spend so much time on social media, there is bound to be an increase in self-esteem issues, depression, anxiety, and insecurity.

"To be human is to have inferiority feelings."

— Renowned Austrian physician and psychiatrist
Alfred Adler (1870-1937)

In this age where so many images of 'perfection' are depicted across many digital platforms, inferior feelings are likely intensified. Worse yet, most people do not realize they are making these comparisons or why they feel so terrible after scrolling through social media. This feeling does not stop the compulsion to check the platforms every chance they get.

To be clear, social comparisons happen in the real world, too. However, this is done on a small scale between us and a few other people we come into contact with.

On social media, social comparison happens on an immeasurable scale as we compare ourselves to potentially millions of other people repeatedly – all in a short period.

The pressures most teens feel from social media (such as their social status and coming into their identity) are consistent with their developmental level. Social media certainly lends itself to comparing ourselves to others regardless of age. Still, it is up to us parents to help our teens recognize this happens and help them find coping techniques. Umbrella condemnations of social media will not help the cause. It might just cause a rift between you and your teen. A more constructive approach is to work with your teen to understand the particular issues that cause them stress via the use of social media. This allows for developing a strategy for social media that tailors use to connect them with their peers best.

The Benefits of Social Media

Distraction. Disruption of healthy sleep patterns. Exposure to online bullies. An unrealistic view of how other people live their lives. Peer pressure. There are many negatives associated with teenage social media use. According to many studies, the negative impact may be related to how much a teen uses social media. In a 2019 study, over 6,500 youngsters in the US aged 12 years to 15 years were assessed. Those who spent more than three hours a day using social media were at a higher risk of developing mental health issues. In the same year, another study featuring 12,000 UK teens aged 13 years to 16 years found that more than three hours of social media use daily was an indication that a teen likely suffered from poor mental health and wellbeing.

Those are not the only studies to link social media usage to anxiety and depression in teens. The higher the social media usage, the more emotionally invested a teen was in the platforms. Also, the more a teen uses social media at night, the greater the level of anxiety and depression suffered by them. This is according to a 2016 study conducted on 450 teens. Just one year before, another study linked the increased risk of developing depression and anxiety to teens seeking feedback online and engaging in social comparison on social media.

A 2013 study on older teens found that when they used social media passively (viewing other people's pictures rather than being active posters of content), they typically experienced a decline in overall life satisfaction. In years before, it was found that undergraduate college students who used Facebook for more prolonged periods strongly believed that other people were happier than they were. On the other end of the spectrum, the less this same age group spent on social media and the more time they spent participating in face-to-face interactions with their friends, the less they adopted the same view. Social media is meant to connect us no matter where we are in the world. However, a study at the University of Pennsylvania found that increased use of popular social media platforms like Instagram and Facebook led to increased feelings of loneliness. At the same time, the opposite was also true – decreased usage led to fewer feelings of loneliness and isolation.

Consumption is not the only worrying part of teens' use of social media. Teens tend to be an impulsive bunch. They might post content without considering the repercussions, like invasions of their privacy and the threat to their physical safety. Those who post might share content they later regret or negatively impact their lives. Examples include personal stories and intimate pictures and videos. The backlash of posting this type of content can lead to being bullied online and in person and harassment. Some teens have even been blackmailed because of what they posted online.

With so many harmful consequences associated with teenagers using social media, it is understandable that so many parents want to ban their teens from accessing the platforms. But let's stop and think about this rationally.

The use of social media is not inherently harmful. Remember that correlation and causation are not synonymous. Anxiety and other mental health conditions like depression can lead to more social media usage as a coping mechanism instead of the other way around. Social media can even be used as a tool to raise awareness about teenage anxiety, leading to the teen becoming more self-aware and more likely to reach out for help to manage the condition.

Every teen's experience with social media varies. While there certainly are negative implications, there are also several advantages to a teen accessing social media. They can be empowered and uplifted by some content. They can connect with people they relate to even if those people live in another country or on another continent. They can become more aware of many issues. Even the falseness of what is portrayed on social media can be brought to their attention this way. Many teens understand that the images they see on social media are manipulated snapshots rather than real-life instances. This knowledge makes them less likely to feel insecure about themselves and their lives.

As a parent, remember that social media is not the only factor that may make teens anxious. It is not the enemy. There is typically a combination of factors. Social media is likely a facilitator of the everyday stresses regular socialization creates. It only differs in size and scale. Just as you need to support the teen through everyday social situations, it is also a must to give that support to help them navigate the realm of digital socialization. After all, social media and other forms of digital interaction are here to stay. If your teen's anxiety symptoms seem to be exacerbated by social media use, pay attention to what is explicitly causing those issues.

What's Triggering about Social Media?

This begs the question. What about social media use may be specifically triggering your teen's anxiety? Let's explore a few of these potentials in this section.

The spike in dopamine

Social media is designed to be addictive. The design seems to have worked because more than 50 percent of teens who use social media think they are addicted. How? Let me explain. No two people see the same content on their social media feeds because the content is curated for individual users by the platform's algorithm. Algorithms are an ever-changing set of rules that rank content on your feed. This rank is based on how likely you are to like and engage with that content. For example, if your teen likes cars, more videos about racing or fixing engines might pop up on his feed. This would contrast with another teen who might like fashion content. Her feed might have content like clothing try-ons and the best earrings to match a particular pair of shoes. The algorithm uses your level of engagement with specific content, like how much you comment, what you like, share, and follow, and your past activity, to design this collection of content.

The way algorithms work, they try to get and keep attention. The reinforcing nature activates the brain's reward center every time your teen goes on the platform by releasing dopamine. This is the same hormone linked to the pleasure we feel because of social interactions, eating food we like, and having sex.

The algorithm emotionally links us to the platforms. *Pew Research Center* reveals 81 percent of US teens use social media. This means that 81 percent of teenage brains are habituated to repeated stimuli on their social media feeds. The unpredictable nature of what they will find whenever they open these apps keeps them returning for more. Think of it like using slot machines. If we knew the outcome every time we pulled the lever down, most people would not play. However, the unknown potential reward keeps many hooked on the game. The same applies to social media. As such, the algorithm places more and more extreme ideas, pictures, and stories in front of your teen's eyes to elicit an emotional response. Teens' beliefs about themselves, their bodies, and even politics can grow incrementally more extreme, almost imperceptibly and unintentionally, as a result. This extreme often perpetuates negatively.

Suppose a teen does not access social media as they are used to. Just like with any other addiction, they will experience feelings of withdrawal like body pains, anxiety, and depression. The teen may feel desperate to access social media to make the emotional and physical distress go away.

FOMO

Fear of missing out (FOMO) describes the apprehension of either missing out on events, experiences, or decisions that might improve their lives or not knowing about such items. Feelings of missing out can develop in a variety of ways. It may be that the teen feels like if they have not joined the social media websites or are not usually active, they may miss out on connections, jokes, discussions, or invitations that come through the platform. They may feel like they need to be in the know, like everyone who uses these platforms. This could prevent them from fitting in with real-life interactions and conversations. They may go on these platforms and see people attending an event or activity they did not know about or were not invited to. Feeling excluded in such ways can lead to feelings of:

- Jealousy
- Worthlessness
- Sadness

To stave off these feelings, teens may find themselves compulsively picking up their phones every few minutes or reaching for the phone every time a notification sounds to ensure they have not missed anything. This compulsion can lead to the teen taking unnecessary risks like scrolling through social media while driving and endangering their health in other ways, like missing out on needed sleep at night or giving social media priority over real-life interactions and relationships.

Feelings of inadequacy about oneself or life

Even knowing that the portrayals on social media are mainly false does not prevent teens from feeling insecure about the things going on (or lack thereof) in their lives or their appearances. Most people do not want to view the low points in other people's lives regularly. It would likely remind us of things we are not too happy about in our own life.

Social media offers an escape from reality. We go there to see the highlights and things that we want to aspire to. However, feelings of envy and dissatisfaction about different aspects of our lives are generally unavoidable as we scroll through pictures of airbrushed bodies and faces, staged videos taken from only flattering angles, and mentions of teens who already own million-dollar businesses while juggling school and an active social life.

Cyberbullying

Cyberbullying is when someone spreads hateful rumors or lies about someone else, sends offensive comments, or posts things the other person cannot control or change. They send texts, pictures, or videos that the other person is uncomfortable with. This form of abuse can leave lasting emotional scars on a teen.

Pressure to post and be engaging

Just as other users of social media influence teens, they can also be influencers. They can post content for other people to see and interact with. With that ability comes pressure to post content that presents them in a light that flatters them and brings that favor from other people using the platform. They want to look attractive in photos and videos. They want to get likes, more followers, and positive comments from their posted content. And what a rush of dopamine comes when they get as desired.

However, putting themselves in the spotlight on social media can lead to not only them being the target of cyberbullying but also feeling that content needs to be better - like they need to be better. Social media serves as a stage of self-presentation. Teens can choose how they present themselves - their character, appearance, life, etc. - to others on these platforms. Whereas face-to-face interactions are subject to other people's perceptions, the online self can be performed down to every last detail. Like other social media influencers, they want to present their ideal selves to the digital world. But there may be a gap between who your teen believes is their ideal self and who they are. A positive association with their ideal self can lead to self-improvement and growth, but feeling like they're failing to live up to their ideal self (especially if this persona is unrealistic) in real life can be a source of emotional turmoil.

In such cases, the production of such content will bring up downward social comparisons to other online personas who seem to have achieved this ideal state. This can easily lead to feelings of inadequacy and insecurity.

How to Protect Your Teen's Mental Health from Social Media

We have established it is not that social media is inherently harmful to teens' mental health, but instead, there may be triggering aspects to its use. Now, let's get into how parents can mitigate anxiety from social media usage without overreacting. It might be your first instinct to take your teen's phone away, especially if you suspect they are engaged in drama on social media, but I urge you to resist the temptation! This will likely cause more harm than good as your teen will feel separated from their friends and missing out. It's understandable to want to separate the youth from the device. Still, my daughter's psychiatrist says that taking her phone away is likely to increase feelings of isolation and depression. Additionally, confiscating the device will prevent you from getting down to the social issues affecting your teen.

Therefore, instead of separating your teen from the device, take an individualized management approach to tackle your teen's issues. To do that effectively, check in with your teen. Find out what's happening in all aspects of their social life, including digitally. Discuss what they are interested in viewing and engaging with on social media. Learn how they interact with their peers on the platforms. As with all situations, there may be areas where there is friction or difficulty. Provide support and offer to help them solve problems when such situations inevitably arise.

After you have adopted such a mentality, tailor your approach using the following tips:

Set limits

The more teens use social media, the more likely they are to develop anxiety and other mental health issues. However, removing the use entirely can, and most likely will, open up a new can of worms. Instead of banning social media, set boundaries for its use. Such limits can include having screen-free periods for scheduled times during the day or on certain occasions. For example, the car ride to school can be used as a screen-free time so that you can talk and catch up distraction-free. Weekends and extended periods like school vacations can also be used as screen-free times. You might be surprised, but many teens appreciate the break. My daughter recently went to a sleepaway camp for a week, and no phones were allowed. She wasn't looking forward to that aspect at first. She said it was hard initially. But she didn't miss her phone after a while and was glad for the break. She was, however, overwhelmed when she returned and faced hundreds of notifications and messages.

Another limit can be having a cut-off time for using social media and devices for the day. An hour or two before your teen goes to bed is a good guide. Encourage them to do something that soothes them, like journaling or reading. Keeping smartphones and other devices out of the teen's bedroom at bedtime encourages a routine that avoids social media use. They might pick up the device without realizing it if it is within easy reach.

The best way to ensure your teen adheres to these limits is to abide by them yourself. Be an example for your children. You can even show your teen that smart devices can be used to engage in real-life interaction, like playing digital games together and sharing video clips, articles, and even memes that you mutually enjoy or are interested in. This invites discussion in real life.

Monitor your teen's social media usage

Sometimes, teens are anxious about their phones because they fear their privacy will be invaded. Do not compound this worry by monitoring your teen's social media usage without their knowledge. Have the discussion and let your teen know you regularly check in (at least once a week) on their accounts. Build consensus and allow them to weigh in on this process. Being controlling will only lead to resistance, or, worse, the teen will hide the actualities of their usage from you.

Once that commitment has been made, ensure you follow through. If anything concerning pops up, be open, nonjudgmental, and communicative. Stick to the schedule for monitoring. Avoid constant surveillance. You don't want the teen to feel like you are always breathing down their neck. Consider setting up a program that allows you to monitor your teenager's phone remotely. We use the Bark app for this purpose, which helps us keep track of the content on our daughter's phone. The app notifies us if it detects any concerning content, such as mental health issues, drug and alcohol use, or bullying. Additionally, the app can track location, manage screen time, and block websites. Our daughter is aware that we use the app to monitor her phone and is comfortable with it.

Discuss social media usage with your teen

Social media can cause disruptions in your teen's life. It can interfere with extracurricular activities, school, homework, and even their eating habits. Discuss these possible adverse outcomes of uncontrolled usage so your teen knows these potential pitfalls. The more aware they are, the faster they can sense if there is a problem with their usage.

Additionally, talk to your teen about what is and is not okay when using social media. Highlight the need to refrain from bullying others, spreading rumors and gossip, and spreading or posting content that can potentially damage someone else's reputation. This goes for both online and offline interactions. Likewise, encourage the teen to report to you or another trusted party if they are on the receiving end of any of these nefarious social media practices.

Apart from these tips, make it a habit to regularly talk to your teen about their encounters on social media. Ask them how they use the platforms, what content caught their attention, and how they feel. Model ethical and mindful social media usage and share those habits with your teen. Finally, routinely remind your teen that social media is full of unrealistic portrayals and that they should be conscious of comparing themselves to others on these platforms.

Encourage interactions with their peers outside of social media

Several studies highlight socialization with face-to-face interaction as great for mental and emotional health and well-being. The parties involved get to see each other as they engage in conversation. Facial expressions and body language can be observed, adding value to the dialogue. When a sense of community is fostered in groups better, stronger relationships are formed, often founded on trust.

Encourage your teen to interact face-to-face with peers as often as possible to gain all the benefits and more. Encourage your teen to join clubs and groups with others who have similar interests. Sports events are always a good suggestion for this as they can provide the physical activity and exercise they need simultaneously. Allow them to do activities like seeing a movie or visiting the beach with friends and peers. Have them volunteer for charity. There are infinite ways to inspire your teen to engage in more physical interactions with others, especially those in the same age group.

Teens were anxious before they started posting on TikTok and scrolling on Instagram. Social media platforms like these can compound feelings of loneliness even if invented to make us more social. They can lead to your teen comparing themselves to others whose content often poses them in an unrealistic light. Teens are pressured to meet unfounded, untrue, and unattainable expectations.

Their digital habits make things worse. They are obsessively following the exploits of filtered and photo-shopped social media influencers. They are responding to text messages around the clock. They are compulsively reaching for their smart devices because ping after ping alerts them to new activity. They get a boost of feel-good chemicals injected into their brains by the actions but then feel poorly about themselves. They might not know it, but they link their self-worth to what they see and post online.

The detrimental effects of social media use on teens can scare many parents. However, banning the use of social media will not take away your teen's anxiety. While there is a link between anxiety in teens and social media use, social media does not cause the condition. Instead, lessen anxiety related to social media use by managing your teen's habits. Use tactics like setting boundaries for the use and modeling the ideal use of the platforms. On the other hand, uncontrolled social media usage can lead to a teen developing thoughts of self-harm or, worse, suicide if the content they see does not nurture good mental health. We will discuss the possibility of teen self-harm and suicide in the next chapter.

Chapter 6
Breaking the Silence: Understanding Teenage Anxiety, Suicide, and Self-Harm

Self-harm is the act of intentionally causing one's self-injury due to being emotionally, mentally, or physically overwhelmed. An individual engaging in self-harm does so to cope with intense feelings. The intent is not to end one's life. Instead, self-harm serves as a means of escape from debilitating thoughts and feelings.

Suicide is different. It is the act of ending one's life, often because of a deep sense of hopelessness. This person cannot see a solution to escaping that pit of despair and feels it is better to escape via that means.

Among teens ages 15 to 19 years, suicide is the third leading cause of death. That is only behind accidents from unintentional injuries and homicide! What a dismal outlook, but it gives insight into the poor state of mental and emotional health in that age group. Suicide attempts in this age range show (with 1 out of 100 suicide attempts being successful) girls were more likely to reach that state of hopelessness. The gender gap is enormous, with a 4 to 1 margin of females to males. While girls tend to think about and attempt suicide more, boys tend to die from attempts more often by at least four times the rate of girls. This is because boys tend to use more lethal means.

A survey found that 8-10 percent of high school students have attempted suicide. The most frequent method of attempt is drug overdose. Luckily (and this by no means diminishes this as a method of attempt), drug overdose tends to be less deadly compared to other ways of attempting suicide. Girls also favored cutting themselves as a method of attempt. The use of a firearm was the most frequent method that led to the completion of the act.

A strong correlation between teen anxiety and thoughts and attempts of suicide exists. The presence of any anxiety disorder (particularly PTSD and panic disorder) increases the risk of a teen thinking about suicide by approximately eight times. It also increases the probability of a suicide attempt by almost six times. It is estimated that the population with anxiety contributes up to 10 percent of suicidality. More than 70 percent of people who admitted to attempting suicide have an anxiety disorder. Teens need help to manage anxiety symptoms so their risk of attempting suicide is reduced.

Our teens need help seeing that there is hope, light beyond the clouds and rain, and life is worth living and fighting for. We need to show them that there are better-coping mechanisms than hurting themselves or, worse, ending their life prematurely when it has so much potential and promise. It is up to us to provide that help and support so they gain insight.

Education is the most powerful tool for doing so. We have first to understand how self-harm and suicide relate to anxiety. We need to understand the risk factors and triggers that cause the development of such thoughts and how these dark thoughts lead to teens acting on them. We need to gain the ability to spot a teen who does self-harm or who thinks about dying by suicide. We need to learn to prevent such acts from happening. Only then can we aid our teens in adopting healthy coping strategies and a more positive outlook.

This chapter is your information kit on these topics and more. Let's dive into it because a teenager's life and health might depend on your knowledge.

Before I do that, though, I must say one thing... As a mother of someone with anxiety and as a human, it was tough to read the facts about teens deliberately injuring themselves and also trying to end their lives. Writing about them and providing the facts to you wrenched my heart just as deeply. You love your child, and just as I do, you would hate to think that they are driven to such drastic measures because of the battles they fight in their mind. But as parents of anxious teens, it is a reality we face, and those are possibilities we must tackle head-on so our children do not become part of these statistics.

Even though your heart will be heavy, I urge you to read this chapter bravely. Be mindful that some of these words may be triggering. If you need to take a breather when it becomes too much, that is more than okay. Come back to these pages when you are calmer. Remember to look for support if you need it. Let's continue together on this journey of helping our teens fight this mental illness with a courageous spirit.

Self-Harm and the Anxious Teen

We all face stressful things. Many of us are working through traumas from the past. Even at a tender age, these truths also apply to your teen. So that we do not become overwhelmed by intense emotions, we use coping techniques. These strategies help us manage these feelings so that their force does not swallow us. Self-harm is a coping mechanism. Self-harming is an attempt to change emotional pain into physical pain. The physical pain may:

- Give the individual a sense of control.
- Help elude traumatic memories.

- Reduce overwhelming thoughts or feelings.
- Provide something tangible to hold onto instead of the invisible force of the emotions.
- Help the individual feel less disconnected, disassociated, or numb.
- Create a reason to engage in physical care.
- Be an expression of suicidal thoughts and feelings without actually going through with them.

The reasons for engaging in self-harm are not limited to only those listed above. Unfortunately, anxiety can lend itself to the development of this unhealthy coping mechanism. An anxiety disorder that causes a teen to resort to self-harm is typically excessive and recurring. Anxiety symptoms fester to such a deplorable condition that the teen needs this mechanism to release the tension.

I love the use of analogies to give a simple, understandable image of the complicated issues in the anxious mind. Envision a covered boiling pot with a roiling liquid that is spilling over. If you remove the lid, the pressure is released, and the temperature is reduced temporarily. As a result, the liquid stops spilling over. However, as long as the lid stays on, the pressure and temperature remain high. The liquid will continue to spill over. The boiling liquid represents overwhelming emotions. The lid is the tension and pressure felt because of the intense feelings. Self-harm offers that temporary release of pressure, like the removal of the lid over a boiling pot.

Self-harm can take many forms: head banging, hitting, or stabbing oneself, hair pulling, cutting, burning, skin picking, or even excessively rubbing the skin. Any such deliberate infliction of injury on oneself without the intention to die by suicide diverts the teen's attention away from the mess of feelings inside to the pain they feel outside their bodies. That physical pain feels more manageable than the emotional burden.

If your teen self-harms, here are the steps you can take to help them find better ways to cope with anxiety:

Control your reaction

Learning that your teen self-harms is distressing. If you are in this situation, you will worry. You might feel helpless and even angry – with yourself, your teen, and the world. You might want to instantly command your teen to stop or demand to know why they are doing this. But you need to reign in these emotions and impulses. Do not make this about you. Of course, your feelings should be felt and honored, but this needs to be done privately when your teen is unaffected.

The focus needs to be on your teen, what they feel, and how you can carefully tend to their feelings to prevent future incidents of this. Most teens who self-harm already feel remorse, guilt, and shame because of their actions. Do not heighten these feelings and make the situation worse by reacting impulsively. Being criticized, feeling attacked, or suffering the brunt of an overreaction from a parent will most likely cause the teen to shut the parent out, isolate, and maybe even engage in more frequent bouts of self-harm.

Keep your wits about you and remain calm. This is a time to explore how your teen feels and why they are pushed to such extremes. There needs to be frank dialogue with open-ended questions. Truly listen to what your teen says so you two can plan the way forward.

Get help

Self-harm is not a condition you can hope goes away. Even though suicide is not the intention of self-harm, it is something that needs to be immediately addressed with the aid of a licensed mental health professional. A teen who engages in self-harm needs individual therapy, where a therapist or psychiatrist will perform a comprehensive evaluation to note the particulars of the teen's struggles. You should seek the help of a therapist or psychiatrist who specializes in working with teens and is trained in cognitive behavioral therapy (CBT). Dialectical behavior therapy (DBT), another talk therapy, may help the teen learn to regulate their feelings and how to implement more positive coping skills. Medication may be prescribed in severe cases.

Work as closely as possible with the teen's therapist so you also learn positive, life-affirming skills that can be incorporated into your household routines. Family therapy should also be considered so that the entire unit learns to improve communication skills and better support each other.

Understand the triggers

Without understanding why this happens, treatment will not be effective. There is no simple, one-size-fits-all answer that will explain why teens are self-harming, though. The reason is always unique to the individual. However, a common thread appears to be the release of tension that is derived when endorphins are released due to feeling the physical pain experienced when inflicting self-injury. This euphoric feeling trumps the emotional numbness or feeling of being overwhelmed previously experienced.

Other feelings often trigger teens into self-harm. Common feelings on the spectrum include:

- Sadness
- Loneliness
- Anger
- Irritability
- Rejection
- Fear

Possible reasons such feelings arise include a response to discord in the family dynamic and social issues. Be mindful that social media may be a facilitator of self-harming. Teens have access to so much information via these mediums. That information can include content like videos and pictures showing other teens self-harming to cope with emotional pain and trauma. Self-harming might even be shown as trendy or something done by the popular crowd. Impressionable teens may consider doing the same to fit in. Anxious teens may cling to these portrayals as hope to fight through intense emotions. They may try to adopt the same coping techniques.

Develop a list of go-to healthy coping strategies

Apart from therapy, the teen must also learn to employ healthier coping mechanisms when stressed. Simple yet effective coping strategies that help with anxiety include meditation, deep and conscious breathing, and yoga. Meditation invites calm and serenity into your teen's mind and life. Deep breaths help your teen work through intensely emotional moments so that they do not resort to unhealthy coping mechanisms such as self-harm. Yoga encourages integrating a mind and body experience so the teen becomes grounded in the here and now rather than other periods that might cause unpleasant memories or worries.

Self-harm is addictive because the act causes a release of feel-good compounds in the brain. Like drug or alcohol use, the teen is urged to do it again and again to feel the pleasure. Therefore, relying on new, healthier coping strategies is something that will take time, just like getting over any other addiction. Ensure a higher chance of successfully transitioning to more constructive coping mechanisms by having several ready and easily accessible. These could include listening to music, talking to friends, writing, drawing, doodling, or watching movies. All these and more can be added to the arsenal of easily done coping techniques.

Over time, teens may see that they enjoy or use some more readily than others. Stick with those, as there will be less mental resistance in times of emotional turmoil. If the teen hates the idea of a particular coping tactic, discard it from the list after a few tries. The first time the teen goes out into nature to self-soothe might feel foreign. The first time they do a yoga session might make them feel silly. The first time they pick up a pencil to doodle, they might feel like they have hit a mental wall. However, being patient and allowing the coping strategy to grow on them is essential. It should be replaced with something new if it still feels wrong after a few tries. It is perfectly okay to jump from using one coping skill to others! This can mean using several in just one day. Playing video games is a common coping strategy for many anxious teen boys, but screen time needs to be limited for good health and well-being. Therefore, the teen might play video games for an hour or two, then move on to listening to music and then taking a walk later.

Manage expectations when using coping skills. They will not be effective every single time or make things magically better. This is something both you and your teen need to understand. Expecting otherwise will lead to displeasure, and the teen will likely fall back into the same destructive pattern of self-harming. Sometimes, they will work wonders; other times, the teen might still feel down in the dumps. The effectiveness will be higher if the teen consistently implements positive coping. The teen should also remember that feeling 25 or 32 percent better beats wallowing in the agony of emotional pain. Just keep at it!

Create a safety plan

The above coping strategies must not just reside in your teen's head. It must be developed in a tangible form to be solidified as a trustworthy source of help. It must be written down and coupled with sources of support. This document is called a safety plan. A safety plan is not just a handy tool to help pull you out of the emotional upheaval of your mind if you have thoughts of harming yourself. It also aids in situations where the individual worries about someone else hurting them or experiencing severe emotional distress. A safety plan certainly aids in keeping your teen physically safe, but it has another purpose. It is also meant to ensure emotional wellness. It increases the chances of both outcomes by addressing each of the following items:

- **Warning signs and triggers** - Outline the things that cause emotional pain and the signs that signal those feelings are being stirred up.
- **Coping mechanisms** - What can you do to work through those feelings or otherwise distract yourself from them if they can't be addressed immediately?
- **Support network** - Who are the people (friends, family, and others) you trust to support and help you through these intense feelings?
- **Professional services** - What are the emergency contacts if a crisis occurs?
- **Social settings** - Outline places you can go so you do not feel alone and the social settings that can provide a temporary escape or outlet when you feel overwhelmed.
- **Safe spaces** - What environment feels like a safe space, and what items can be added or removed to ensure this zone remains a retreat and sanctuary?
- **Life-affirming reasons** - What are some reasons it is good to be alive? What are the things and people you care about most?

I recommend getting a journal and creating boxes that can be filled in for the six items above. This makes developing a safety plan a cinch. Completing this plan must be done before a crisis occurs. It works because it shows the teen there is motivation to live a healthy life with constructive ways to handle stress. It shows them people care about them and who they can contact for help. It shows them they can gain control even during intense emotional storms.

The answers to the items addressed above will change as time passes. Therefore, a system of periodic reviews must be set up to update the plan.

Be emotionally supportive

Replacing the unhealthy coping strategies of self-harm with more adaptive ones will be difficult. Your teen needs your support through the transition. They need you to be empathetic and compassionate. Make time to connect with the youngster one-on-one. Both of you need to slow down from packed schedules, if applicable, to develop this connection.

Other ways you can lend this emotional shoulder include:

- Encouraging the teen to connect frequently with a positive, supportive network that includes friends and other adults, like the school counselor and family members
- Implementing relaxation techniques like walking, venturing into nature, and integrating mindfulness apps into their daily and weekly routines
- Exercising and doing physical activities
- Creating a list of people the teen can call anytime if they feel overwhelmed

There may be times when your teen rejects your support. Be patient and continue to validate your teen's feelings and pain, even if only with your sturdy presence. Self-harm is a highly triggering topic to discuss, especially with one's parents. However, the teenager must learn to mindfully and objectively observe the inner dialogue that leads to self-harm. Such thoughts can be a response to stressors experienced because of interactions with peers at school, and in other areas in the teen's life. No matter how trivial it can seem to someone else, these stressors can cause severe psychological pressure. Awareness is always the first step to managing and treating any decline in mental health.

Expect your teen not to want to share their innermost thoughts with you. Do not be offended by this. The thoughts that lead to self-harm are highly personal. The teen might be ashamed or embarrassed about these thoughts. They might not know how to express these thoughts or feelings to you. No matter the reason, be patient. Be supportive. Refrain from pressing, but keep offering your teen the chance to unburden themselves.

Your child must release these thoughts and feelings even if not with you. Encourage them to get them out of their head and into a more easily examined form, such as writing them in a journal or sketching them onto a sketch pad. A common CBT practice is using a tool called a thought diary. This is a journal where anxious thoughts, along with the resulting behaviors, are documented.

How to Tell If Your Teen is Engaging in Self-Harm

To get a self-harming teen the help they need means knowing how to spot the signs. Most people who self-harm do not seek help. Like other age groups, a self-harming teen will likely be skilled at hiding the practice from people around them, even people close to them, like their parents. If your teen suffers from anxiety, particularly severe anxiety, it is up to you to look for the signs that self-harm might be occurring. The most obvious sign is suspicious marks or scars on the teen's legs, arms, or torso.

The signs may be more subtle. They include:

- Wounds that do not heal or get worse as time passes
- Wounds that the teen does not have a reasonable explanation for obtaining

- Mentions of or talking about self-harm. The teen will likely refrain from speaking to their parents or other adults about this. However, they might be more open with peers. As such, you must develop relationships with your teen's friends and their parents. While their peers may not come to you with such concerning references, they may mention it to their parents, who can bring it to your attention. Alternatively, apps like Bark, mentioned in the previous chapter, can monitor your teenager's texts for mentions of self-harm or suicidality.
- Being secretive
- The collection of sharp objects
- Wearing long-sleeved tops or long pants constantly, even in hot weather
- Frequently wearing bandages
- Avoiding activities where they might have to change clothes in front of other people. Sporting activities are an example of where this may occur.
- Being anti-social and isolating

While some of these indications can lend themselves to other possible causes, it is better to investigate and find a lesser worry than to let things slide only to learn about such behavior when the situation has deteriorated to the point where the teen needs to be hospitalized or worse.

Are Self-Injury and Suicide Linked?

UK's National Health Service reports that more than 50 percent of the people who die as a result of suicide have a history of engaging in self-harm. However, engaging in self-harm is different from an attempt at one's own life. Self-harm is often an intent to punish oneself, to relieve tension that seems unbearable, or as a form of expressing the terrible despair that resides in this person's mind rent-free. The reason for inflicting intentional pain is often a mixture of all these reasons. No matter what the reason is, self-harm is an effort to unburden the load of overwhelming emotions. It is a path taken to escape a more bearable pain whose source can't be seen. It is a way to cope with the pressures of life.

Self-harm and its rationales can be related to but are different from the mental pathways that lead to suicide attempts. Still, people who self-harm risk their lives because the outcome can be fatal. Dirty objects used for cutting into the skin can lead to infections. Cutting too deeply can slice into an artery or vein and lead to uncontrolled bleeding. Breaking bones and setting fires can be taken too far. Swallowing non-food items can lead to choking and problems with the digestive system. Not only can self-harming become a deadly practice, but it can also lead to developing suicidal thoughts. While teens might initially self-harm without any intention of ending their lives, developing suicidal thoughts is not a massive leap if the teen's mental health deteriorates further.

But what leads to a teen developing suicidal thoughts, or worse, acting on these thoughts? Let's discuss these pressing questions next.

Risk Factors for Suicide in Adolescence

Teens who are considering suicide may engage in a range of behaviors, including but not limited to:

- Discussing suicide or death in general
- Hints that they might not be around for much longer
- Expressing feelings of hopelessness or guilt
- Isolating themselves from friends and family
- Writing about death, separation, and loss through mediums like songs, letters, and poems
- Giving away prized possessions suddenly

- Loss of interest in previously enjoyed activities, school, or sports
- Difficulty focusing or thinking coherently
- Changes in appetite or sleep patterns
- Engaging in risky behaviors like driving too fast

The reasons why a teen would contemplate, let alone attempt suicide, are highly complex and unique to that individual. However, the relationship between social, biological, genetic, and psychological factors plays a huge role in determining the youngster's risk for suicidal tendencies. While there is no way of knowing the exact thought patterns that lead to teen suicide, we can look at the different risk factors that increase the chances. With knowledge, we can develop strategies for prevention.

These risk factors include:

Personality traits

Suicide is often associated with impulsiveness. The transition from thoughts of suicide to dying by suicide often occurs suddenly and unexpectedly. This is particularly common among adolescents with weaker problem-solving skills and a passive attitude toward dealing with problems.

Some studies also suggest that this may be due to defects in memory, perfectionism, and a rigid thinking process that cannot consider nuances and gradations. This can lead to:

- Insecurity
- Lack of conviction
- Low self-esteem
- Poor anger management
- Aggression

CBT-based interventions, such as ACT, may help address these issues and improve mood regulation and problem-solving skills.

Mental disorders

The majority of studies suggest that suicide is closely linked to the presence of mental disorders. Approximately 90 percent of individuals who die by suicide experience at least one mental disorder. Mental disorders have been found to contribute 47-74 percent to the risk of suicide, with affective disorders being the most common disorder found in this context. An affective disorder, like depression, refers to a mental health disorder involving disturbances in a person's mood. Depression, specifically, is present in 50-65 percent of suicide cases, with a higher prevalence among females than males. With higher numbers in older teens and males, people with substance abuse, particularly alcohol misuse, have an elevated risk of dying by suicide. Like the other mental disorders listed, there is a strong connection between anxiety disorders and suicide.

It is essential to recognize, however, that the majority of individuals with mental health conditions do not die by suicide.

Previous suicide attempts

Between 25 and 33 percent of all cases of suicide occur after an earlier attempt of the action, with the occurrence being more predominant in boys than girls. Boys who previously attempted suicide are 30 times more at risk moving forward compared to boys with no previous attempts. Girls have three times the risk after an earlier attempt. Studies show that 1-6 percent of people who previously attempted suicide die by suicide within the first year after the initial attempt. Previous suicide attempts are a risk factor for future suicide attempts because they indicate a history of suicidal behavior. Additionally, a history of suicide attempts can also contribute to a person's feelings of hopelessness and despair, which are common precursors to suicidal thoughts and behaviors.

Factors relating to family

The family setting plays a crucial role in supporting youngsters through their challenges. As such, family structure and processes are linked to suicidal behavior in youth. Half of all youth suicide cases have family factors as a contributor to the act. A family history of mental disorders, particularly depression and substance abuse, has strong ties to youth attempts. Studies are inconclusive as to whether family mental disorders directly influence adolescent suicidal behavior or if they indirectly impact teenagers through mental disorders caused by family circumstances.

There are also high statistics of suicidal behavior among teens whose family members have died by suicide. Why this happens is still unclear. It may be imitation behavior by the teen, but it has been found that there is a more significant link between suicidal behavior and biological relatives compared to adoptive relatives. These findings suggest a genetic connection. This is also consistent with numbers highlighting suicidal behavior in teens with parents who attempted suicide in the past without the teen's knowledge. Both genetics and imitation may be at play.

It is not only genetics and imitation that link the family to teen suicide risk. Other family factors include:

- Poor communication about the teen's mental issues, as well as in general between family members
- Direct conflicts with parents
- Violence at home

Parental divorce also has a weak association with teen suicide. This correlation is likely the result of the practical, financial, and socioeconomic implications of living in a single-parent family, co-parenting issues, or the background factors that led to the separation.

Specific life events

Youth suicide rates are often linked to significant life events, such as personal losses, school problems, and conflicts with parental figures. These stressors can significantly impact young people still trying to establish their identity and build self-confidence. Research shows that peer rejection, romantic break-ups, and the death of friends are associated with 20 percent of youth suicide cases. Additionally, problems at school and stress related to academic performance were found in 14 percent of suicide cases. Teens who feel like they're drifting through life or who lack structure and predictability in their lives have a substantially higher risk of attempting suicide.

Other significant stressors associated with youth suicide include bullying, cyberbullying, mental and physical abuse, and disciplinary trouble with the police. These factors are more common among youth with substance abuse disorders. The behavior of others can influence teens, and they may imitate suicidal behavior. This can happen at a macro level, such as through mass media, or a micro level, like through direct contact with their environment. Imitation effects may depend on the teen's characteristics, how the act is reinforced, and how the act is presented. In some cases, this imitation behavior can lead to suicide clusters. This is a chain of suicides among adolescents in a specific area and period.

Availability of the means to make the attempt

People who are considering suicide often haven't taken a firm stance on the decision. They have mixed feelings about going through with it. In times of terrible stress, such as during the COVID-19 pandemic, the impulse to act on these thoughts can be strong, especially among young people. The availability of means to die by suicide, such as guns or medication, can play a crucial role in the decision to act on these thoughts. In some cases, the method chosen can determine the lethality of the action and may even reflect national patterns in suicide methods. For example, younger age groups may die by suicide by hanging, jumping from a high place, or running into traffic, while adolescents may hang, or use poison or firearms.

Some studies have shown that restricting access to means of suicide can be an effective prevention strategy. The recent increase in gun ownership during the pandemic has been linked to a rise in suicides by women and children living in those homes. In addition to physical availability, cognitive availability, such as media reports or internet information about suicide methods, can also play a role in youth suicide.

Overdose through the use of over-the-counter and prescription medication is common in both attempted and death by suicide. It is recommended to monitor all medicines in the home; if not, lock them up. I have all medications in our house in a cute pink lock box purchased through Amazon, so I do not have to have that worry hanging over my head. Also, note that teens may trade or carry prescription drugs with them.

Other Risk Factors

Other noteworthy factors that may increase a teen's risk of attempting suicide include:

Being part of the LGBTQ (lesbian, gay, bisexual, or any other sexual minority) community

Let's clear a possible misconception right off the bat - LGBTQ youth are not inherently more likely to experience suicidal thoughts or behaviors because of their sexual orientation or gender identity. Instead, they are placed at higher risk because of the discrimination, stigma, and mistreatment they face in society. This is evident in the findings of the *Trevor Project's 2022 National Survey on LGBTQ Youth Mental Health*, which showed that LGBTQ teens are at a higher risk of suicide. These findings were supported by recording the experiences of about 34,000 LGBTQ youth aged 13 to 24 years in the US.

The factors that support this elevated risk include:

- Minority stress like internalized homophobia, discrimination, and a lack of understanding or acceptance from others
- Rejection by family, friends, or communities and lack of social support and affirming spaces like LGBTQ-friendly schools or support groups
- Physical harm and bullying with methods like verbal or physical harassment, assault, or even murder
- Discrimination in many areas, including employment, education, and healthcare
- Conversion therapy which is a psychologically harmful and ineffective practice that attempts to change an individual's sexual orientation or gender identity

The survey included a significant number of LGBTQ youth of color (45%) and transgender or nonbinary youth (48%). The results emphasized the need for increased support and protection for LGBTQ youth to address the negative impacts of societal mistreatment and stigma.

And how could the results be anything different when the statistics are this heartbreaking? Half of LGBTQ teens (ages 13–17) seriously thought about attempting suicide in the past year, with 18 percent going through with it. This is more than twice the rate of suicide attempts among all US teens, which sits at 9 percent. Nearly three-quarters of LGBTQ teenagers showed signs of anxiety in the past year, while over half experienced symptoms of depression. A large majority of LGBTQ youth surveyed expressed a need for mental healthcare, but a significant portion was unable to access it. Estimates indicate that over 1.8 million LGBTQ youth seriously consider attempting suicide each year.

The *Trevor Project* reports that at least one LGBTQ youth attempts suicide every 45 seconds.

We need to protect our LGBTQ teens by doing all we can to lower these dreadful odds. The truth is undeniable - LGBTQ youth who have supportive adults and peers in their lives are less likely to attempt suicide. Creating affirming spaces and activities, particularly at school, can also reduce the risk of suicide among LGBTQ youth. Supporting transgender and nonbinary youth with policies and practices that affirm their gender identity can significantly decrease the risk of suicide. Allowing them to change their gender marker on legal documents officially and providing access to affirming spaces can have a positive impact on their mental health. Respecting their pronouns is also associated with lower rates of suicide. Providing gender-affirming medical care, such as hormone therapy, has been shown to improve mental health and reduce the risk of suicide among transgender and nonbinary youth.

Being adopted

Teens who are adopted are four times more likely to attempt suicide.

This is the statistic highlighted by a study of more than 1,200 Minnesota teens. It showed that over 8 percent of adopted girls and 5 percent of boys had attempted to take their own lives, compared to less than 2 percent of non-adopted kids. However, the lead researcher stressed that parents should not be overly alarmed, as most of these adopted children were "psychologically well-adjusted." It is speculated that adopted children may have a higher risk of mental health issues due to a higher rate of psychiatric conditions in their biological parents or due to difficulties with social adjustment.

Adopted kids need to feel a sense of belonging and acceptance within the family. Parents of adopted children are advised to listen to them, be openly communicative, and be aware of any potential problems.

Additionally:

- Help the child develop healthy coping mechanisms for stress and emotional challenges.
- Note potential triggers for suicide like previous trauma or abuse, the presence of mental health disorders, and the teen displaying social isolation.
- Encourage the child to express their emotions and feelings openly and provide them with a safe space to do so.
- Help the child connect with other adopted children and adolescents with similar experiences and challenges.

What to do if you suspect your teen is suicidal

Tackle issues of suspected suicidal thoughts head-on. If you ask someone with purple hair if they have purple hair, they will say yes. They say no if they don't have and don't desire purple hair. You won't make them want purple hair. If they wish to have purple hair or currently have purple hair and are trying to hide it, they will likely be interested or willing to talk about it. We can apply this analogy to talking about teen suicide. Just like asking someone if they have purple hair, using the word "suicide" in conversation with your teen won't plant the idea in their head. It may provide them an opening to express their thoughts and feelings.

It's essential to listen to your teenager and not dismiss their problems. Let them know that you love them and are there to support them through whatever they're going through. Encourage them to talk to a medical professional who can give them the guidance they need. A psychiatrist or psychologist with experience treating children and adolescents with mental health issues can provide a thorough evaluation and recommend the appropriate treatment plan.

Don't ignore warning signs of suicide. Seek help immediately, even if it means making frequent doctor's appointments or seeking residential treatment. Your teenager's mental health is worth the extra attention and care.

There are free resources available. If you are concerned that your teenager is in danger, do not hesitate to contact emergency services. Dial 911, your local emergency number, or a suicide hotline, such as the *National Suicide Prevention Lifeline* at 1-800-273-TALK (1-800-273-8255) in the U.S.

The *988 Suicide & Crisis Lifeline* is available 24/7 and can be reached by calling 1-800-273-8255, texting or calling 988, or contacting them through their website: https://988lifeline.org/. If it is a concern, they will not automatically call the police just for stating that you or your teenager are feeling suicidal. Only if someone expresses that they have the means to die by suicide and intends to do it now and cannot be talked out of it are the police called.

The Trevor Lifeline is also available for the LGBTQ community at 1-866-488-7386 or by texting START to 678678. You can also reach out to them through their website: https://www.thetrevorproject.org/.

These toll-free lines are staffed by trained professionals who can provide confidential support. If the situation is urgent, do not hesitate to call 911 for immediate assistance.

What can you do to prevent teen suicide?

Age is irrelevant. Suicide can be prevented. To prevent teen suicide, it is vital to take proactive steps like:

- Have open and honest discussions about mental health and suicide.

- Pay attention to warning signs, and don't dismiss threats of suicide as "teen melodrama."
- Encourage your teen to spend time with supportive friends and family and not isolate themselves.
- Monitor and discuss your teen's social media use.
- Support a healthy lifestyle by encouraging regular exercise, a healthy diet, and adequate sleep.
- Provide support for any treatment plan for suicidal behavior and encourage participation in activities that can boost confidence.
- Seek the help of a therapist or counselor for family therapy or cognitive behavioral treatment.
- Monitor medication usage and be aware of any potential increase in suicidal thoughts or behavior.
- Safely store firearms, alcohol, and medications to limit access to potential means of self-harm. This is the most evidence-based advice! Be willing to lock up your medications if your teenager is using them or intends to. Be willing to get rid of your gun or store it outside of the home if your child is at risk of suicide. Doing so is effective in preventing deaths by suicide.

If you are worried about your teen's mental health, it is essential to take action and seek help immediately.

Parenting is no walk in the park, and it is not made easier by the issues we have discussed thus far in this book. But you've got this! The next chapter will provide that extra assistance you can rely on to make an even better go at it.

Chapter 7

Guiding Through the Storm: Parenting Teenagers with Anxiety

As the years pass, our children evolve, taking on different personalities and characteristics. Parents of teenagers often experience a range of emotions due to the unique challenges and changes that come with raising a budding adult. These emotions can include frustration, worry, and fear. Frustration arises when conflicts develop because teenagers challenge rules and boundaries. Dealing with mood swings and hormonal changes doesn't make it any easier to rein in the exasperation. We worry about their safety, well-being, and future prospects. Fear can slide like a cold grip around our throats when we are concerned about risky behavior, peer pressure, and other potential sources of harm to our teenagers.

It can be difficult not to let these emotions cloud our judgment. As our worries take over, we may say things to our teens or do things we later regret. We may try to handle them with kid gloves for their safety and happiness. But they are no longer kids. We must recognize that our children are no longer babies but young adults who still need comfort and reassurance.

In dealing with anxious adolescents, we often try to make difficult situations more manageable for our children. We want to control outcomes and keep them happy, but this approach is flawed and will likely lead to teen rebellion. Instead, we need to help our teens develop resilience by allowing them to figure it out independently. This is not easy, as our instinct is to protect them and make it all better. But for our children to grow into strong, independent adults, we must let go and trust them to handle challenges to the best of their abilities – with our ever-present support and guidance when required.

While there is no failsafe method to go about parenting a teen with anxiety, this chapter serves as an accumulation of a few guidelines on what to do and what not to do. These strategies will help smooth the rough journey ahead.

The Don'ts

Don't overwhelm the teen with emotional displays

Teenagers can be unpredictable when it comes to their emotions. They tend to shut down when we express our own emotions, often leading to difficulty maintaining conversations with them or having them carry out instructions.

This can be a difficult adjustment for parents. Our big, bold emotions, like showing our excitement and enthusiasm, used to bring our children joy when they were younger. But the rules changed as they entered teenagerhood. We need to keep our sizeable, bold emotions to ourselves. Try to be more subdued to align more with this phase of life.

Don't make your teen fearful of uncertainty

The brain loves to have steps A, B, and C through to Z mapped out beforehand. However, there are times when we don't know what will happen next, so we can't prepare. We have to wing it at the time. This can be a source of great anxiety for teens. You might be tempted to say, "Stop worrying. Everything will be fine." You might even be tempted to make promises in the heat of the moment to take away that worried look on their faces. The need to comfort and remove the mental load of worry is enormous.

However, uncertainty is part of life. The teen needs to learn to deal with the constancy of that fact. Trying always to take away the uncertainty now will only lead to greater levels of anxiety, especially as the teen grows into an adult. You will only sometimes be around to take away the burden, and they need to learn to carry it efficiently on their own.

Instead, if your teen is worried about something, try saying, "It's okay to feel anxious. Let's take a deep breath and focus on the present moment. We don't know what the future holds, but we can trust that we will figure it out together."

Also, never make promises that you may not be able to keep. This will only add to your child's worry and disappointment and cause them to trust you less to keep your word.

Let them know that you are there to support them, but also encourage them to be realistic and adaptable in the face of uncertainty.

Don't always try to fix their problems

When our teenagers face a challenge or a problem, they often ask us for help. Our instinct is to give them advice or solve the issue for them. But jumping in and fixing every taxing situation does not help them develop problem-solving skills. It may alleviate our anxiety, but it does not benefit our teenagers. They gain experience and confidence in handling difficult situations by letting them go through the process themselves.

This is a challenging shift for us as parents. We want to protect our children and keep them safe, but sometimes, we must step back and let them learn independently. While this may cause short-term discomfort, it will ultimately lead to their ability and confidence to handle problems independently.

Don't try to coordinate every detail of your teen's life

We parents want our children to be included in social media photos and real-life events. We know the fear of missing out that our teens sometimes feel, and sometimes, we, too, share the feeling. As a result, many parents carefully plan every aspect of their adolescent's social life. This can lead to teens not knowing how to make social plans or develop new friendships without outside help.

The Dos

Do ask the right questions

How you communicate with your teen can either unite you or build a rift between you. Teens are trying to be more independent, so cater your talks with them to reflect your respect for that transition. Asking questions can be particularly challenging for some parents. Their words can come off as controlling. So, instead of demanding to know who your teen is going out with, where they are going, or what they will be doing, try asking questions that encourage them to make firm decisions and solve problems. Examples of these questions include:

- "Do you have an idea of what to do?"
- "What options have you thought of?"
- "Has anything like this ever happened to you before?"

With such questions, you signal your teen to trust their ability to handle the situation. You are also encouraging them to trust their instincts.

Do validate their emotions and experiences

As a parent, wanting to improve things for your teen is natural. It is also the go-to instinct to give them positive feedback to help them feel better. However, there are more effective approaches than this. Instead, try offering empathy and validation by providing specific and genuine praise when they make progress with problem-solving with words like:

- "I'm sorry. That sounds like a tough situation."
- "It sounds like you handled that situation well."
- "I am happy you have made time to study for your upcoming math test every night."

Also, validate your teen's feelings and tell them how much you care about them. Say things like:

- "I care about you and your safety."
- "You are important to me, and I love you."
- "You are enough, just the way you are."

Raising a teenager can be challenging, but the reward of watching them grow into confident and capable adults is worth it. By offering empathy, validation, and specific praise, we can support our children as they navigate the ups and downs of adolescence.

Do acknowledge your teen's feelings

It's crucial to recognize your teen's anxiety. Even if it's about an unlikely event, it is valid. Instead of telling them not to worry, assure them they can handle it. For instance, if your child is worried about passing an exam, let them know that you understand their concern but are confident in their ability to do their best.

We used to play the "what if" game with my daughter when she was younger. We would take an activity she was anxious about and ask her what would happen if that anxious thought were to come true. Once, we were going through the questions with many family members present. She went through question after question. In the end, her response was, "The building would blow up, and we would all die!"

That made everyone laugh hysterically at the absurdity of her response. She was laughing, too, and the tension was broken. We made sure to reassure her that her worry about the building blowing up was not likely and why to make sure she was less concerned with that possibility. It turned out she was hamming it up for the audience more than anything.

Acknowledging and supporting teens' emotions will help them feel heard and understood. Showing warmth and compassion when doing this teaches the teen how to use self-compassion in difficult situations, which will help them navigate challenges better and cope with difficult emotions more easily.

Do encourage teens to talk about their anxieties openly

By discussing the things that cause anxiety with your child, you can help reduce the amount of anxiety they feel. This open communication also allows you to understand better what is causing their anxiety and how to support them best. Instead of trying to fix the issue, focus on providing coping skills and self-care exercises that can help your child manage their anxiety.

Do highlight how important it is to help other people

Participation in activities that benefit others can improve a teenager's self-esteem and provide a productive, healthy distraction from anxiety. Parents can encourage their teens to volunteer in the community for causes they care about. Joining a group or club with other teens with similar interests can also enhance social skills and create a sense of belonging.

Do be mindful of your expectations of your teen

High expectations and the pressure to succeed can sometimes overwhelm teenagers. Setting realistic goals allows them to focus on improving academically without feeling additional stress about their grades and test scores. This can help them manage their anxieties *and* improve their academic performance.

Do encourage your teen to be brave

To help your teen overcome their anxiety, gently encourage them to set small goals for overcoming things that make them anxious. Avoid pushing them to face situations they are not ready for, though. For example, if your child is anxious about performing in front of others, suggest they practice in front of the family before building up to larger groups.

To help your teen be brave, encourage them to use positive self-talk, self-compassion, and assertiveness. Praise them for attempting something that makes them anxious, no matter how small it may seem.

As a parent, it is crucial to be a good role model in managing your anxiety. Let your child know it is expected to feel anxious sometimes and share your experiences and how you coped with them.

Do help your teen feel safe and secure

To help your teenager cope with the challenges and anxiety of adolescence, create a sense of safety and security for them. Some ways to do this include spending quality time together, having a consistent family routine that includes time for relaxation and socialization, and surrounding them with trusted and supportive individuals. By fostering a sense of safety and security, your child will be better equipped to handle the daily stresses of adolescence.

How to Help a Teenager Through a Panic Attack

Dealing with panic attacks is a reality for parents who have a teen with panic disorder. When a panic attack occurs, remember that it is a natural and valid reaction. The racing heart. Sweating. Shaking. Dizziness. Shortness of breath. Nausea. The symptoms may make the teen believe they are dying or going crazy.

Some parents are frightened by their child's panic attack symptoms, leading them to make anxiety-induced statements like "You are scaring me." Others believe the adolescent is seeking attention. The latter group may either walk away from the teen during the episode or make comments like, "Snap out of it."

I believe the majority of parents raising teens who suffer from panic attacks want to help but don't know how to do so.

The best long-term solution is to seek professional help. While one panic attack does not necessarily require intervention, it is uncommon for people to experience just one attack without others or high levels of anxiety in general.

If your teen is having a panic attack, accept their perceptions and emotions. Even if their fears and reactions are illogical to you, their anxiety is legitimate, so validate their experience. Use statements like "I can see that you are overly anxious, and I am here to support you in any way I can."

When the teen is calm again, ask what they would find helpful. Some may want to be left alone. If that is true, respect their wishes and allow them a moment of privacy. Others may want you to sit quietly with them. Allow them to find comfort in your presence if that is the case.

With their permission, encourage the teen to use either of the following strategies to cope with panic attacks:

T.I.P.P. - Temperature, Intense exercise, Paced breathing, and Paired muscle relaxation

The method focuses on four skills that can help decrease emotional arousal and decrease the activity of the parasympathetic nervous system, which is activated during intense stress or danger. Follow these steps:

- **Tip the temperature** of the face with cold water or ice, either by placing the face in a bowl of cold water for 30-60 seconds or using more moderate methods such as splashing cold water on the eyes and cheeks or using an ice pack.
- Do **intense aerobic activity** for 20 minutes to increase heart rate and decrease anxiety. Examples of this could include running, jumping jacks, or push-ups. Doing this activity with the teen can help provide support and show them they aren't being judged.
- Practice **paced breathing** by slowly inhaling and exhaling five or six breath cycles per minute. Notice the sensation of the breath moving through the abdomen. Focus on making your exhales longer than your inhales. This last part is essential.
- Practice **paired muscle relaxation** by tensing and releasing muscle groups while focusing on the sensations of tension and relaxation and breathing in and out.

T.I.P.P. can be enhanced through the use of guided meditation apps.

The 5-4-3-2-1 method

The technique helps the teen focus on their surroundings and the present moment rather than getting caught up in the anxiety of a panic attack. This grounding practice distracts from negative thoughts and emotions and refocuses attention on the physical sensations in the environment. Encourage your teen to use their senses to list things in their current environment with this methodology:

- 5 things they hear
- 4 things they see
- 3 things they can touch
- 2 things they can smell
- 1 thing they can taste

Additionally, encourage your teen to notice the little things around them that they may need to pay more attention to, such as the patterns in the carpet or the sounds of a passing vehicle.

While neither T.I.P.P. skills nor the 5-4-3-2-1 method cure panic attacks, they can be effective in helping to reduce the teen's immediate distress and discomfort. By learning these techniques and practicing them regularly, the teen can learn to manage their anxiety and cope with panic attacks more effectively. Doing the practices with your teen communicates that they are not alone during the ordeal.

Embracing Resilience: Thriving Beyond Teenage Anxiety

Occasional stints of anxiety are a standard part of the life of an adult. Teenagers face many stressors that cause worry, unease, and distress despite being younger. Teenage anxiety is distinct in several ways. Teenagers are at a critical stage of development where they are becoming more independent and facing new life challenges and pressures. This can make them more susceptible to anxiety and stress. While anxiety is normal, when there is a constant state of worry and apprehension, it is a sign that your child is facing a problem.

Unfortunately, teens are likely to have a hard time recognizing and managing their anxiety symptoms. They may not know how or where to turn to for help and support. This may lead to them engaging in risky behaviors, such as substance abuse and self-harm, as a way of coping with their anxiety. Their thoughts may even deteriorate to such an extent that they contemplate or attempt suicide.

It is up to us parents to help manage our teen's anxiety symptoms with constructive coping mechanisms. Our task has not been made easy. Many factors amplify anxiety in teens in this modern age. The

COVID-19 pandemic has disrupted the normalcy of teenagers' lives. It limited social interactions, caused school closures that disrupted the routine and structure of their lives, and created health concerns and economic uncertainty due to widespread job losses and financial insecurity, which affected them and their families. Increased levels of anxiety among teens are a consequence of that.

Social media, something we did not have to deal with in the past, has been a facilitator of increased teen anxiety rates. Factors like the constant pressure to present a perfect image on social media, the fear of missing out on experiences that friends are sharing, and the potential for cyberbullying and other forms of online harassment have led to this increase.

It seems rather hopeless for teens when there are so many elements increasing teen anxiety and the severity of symptoms.

But there is hope.

We can overcome teen anxiety together.

We can use therapies like ACT (Acceptance and Commitment Therapy), a type of cognitive behavioral therapy. Talk therapy focuses on helping teens accept their thoughts and feelings without judging or trying to change them. In the context of treating anxiety in adolescents, ACT involves teaching them strategies to accept and manage their anxious thoughts and emotions without avoiding or suppressing them.

We can empower them to develop a new normal even as we recover from the COVID-19 pandemic. We can show them what it means to worry productively and how they can take control of their worries when the path is unproductive.

We can show them how to use social media as a beneficial tool that connects them with positive people and nourishes their minds with information rather than allowing it to be a platform where negative social comparisons occur.

Parenting is not easy. It does not come with a guide or manual; every child is unique. The task's difficulty is compounded when the child battles mental health conditions.

As parents, it is natural to feel emotional and worried about our teenagers. This can sometimes lead us to say and do the wrong things, and we want to overcompensate by wrapping them in a blanket and tucking them away from anything that might cause them distress. However, we need to recognize that our children are no longer babies; they are young adults capable of handling difficult situations. They simply need the tools to do so.

Our love and concern may drive us to try to control situations and make them easier for our teenagers. Still, this approach does not foster resilience and grit – mental devices needed to overcome anxiety. Instead, we must allow our teens to figure things out independently and provide support and guidance as needed. We must let go of the inclination to kiss and make it better. The focus needs to be on helping our adolescents develop the skills and confidence to handle life's challenges because challenges will remain a part of their lives as anxiety sufferers. Anxiety cannot be cured, but it can be managed. This book, and *Taming Teenage Anxiety with CBT and DBT,* that I also wrote on the subject, gives you the instruments for management.

The words contained within this book will not miraculously cure your child's anxiety. It would be a false promise to guarantee this. However, it does provide the framework for taking a proactive approach to help your teen overcome anxiety. Consistent effort and digging deep to find what works best for your teen and their particular symptoms can improve their daily life. They can take control of their actions no matter the thoughts and feelings they battle. Don't allow these words to just sit on these pages. Use the tools provided and take the steps toward a happier, healthier, and more fulfilled future for your teen, yourself, and the rest of your family.

Many teens suffer from anxiety, and many family units are shaken because of the fallout. These teens and their families need help to get through these dark hours, and you can help them with a tiny act. If you find this book helpful, please consider leaving a review on Amazon to extend that helping hand. With just a few minutes, you can help the algorithm recognize that this book provides value to families like yours. Just as you have found relief and solutions in these pages, perhaps they can, too. Thank you for reading this book to the end and for supporting others. All the best of luck in helping your teen overcome anxiety!

Passing on the Torch

Spreading Hope and Knowledge for Teenage Anxiety

Congratulations on completing "Taming Teenage Anxiety with ACT"! Now that you're equipped with valuable insights and strategies, it's time to share your experience and help others in their journey toward mental well-being.

By leaving an honest review of this book on Amazon, you're not only sharing your thoughts but also guiding other readers who may be seeking similar support. Your review can be a beacon of hope for teenagers and their families who are navigating the challenges of anxiety.

Thank you for contributing to the sharing of mental health techniques for adolescents. Our joint efforts will ensure that those who need help with teenage anxiety will receive it.

Click here to leave your review on Amazon: https://www.amazon.-com/review/review-your-purchases/?asin=B0D4V3QRBJ

Or scan the QR code below:

Your support is invaluable and greatly appreciated.

Best wishes,

Lillian Middleton

Bibliography

About Teen Suicide (for Parents) - Nemours KidsHealth. (n.d.). https://kidshealth.org/en/parents/suicide.html

ACT for the Public | Association for Contextual Behavioral Science. (n.d.). https://contextualscience.org/act_for_the_public

Alisa Crossfield, Ph.D. (2020, April 27). *How can I help my teen during a panic attack?* Psychology Today. https://www.psychologytoday.com/us/blog/emotionally-healthy-teens/202004/how-can-i-help-my-teen-during-panic-attack

Amy Norton, & Amy Norton. (2013, September 9). *Adopted teens more likely to attempt suicide, study finds.* Healthday-en. https://www.healthday.com/health-news/general-health/adopted-teens-more-likely-to-attempt-suicide-study-finds-679965.html

Anderson, M. (2023, December 11). *Teens, Social Media & Technology 2018 | Pew Research Center.* Pew Research Center: Internet, Science & Tech. https://www.pewresearch.org/internet/2018/05/31/teens-social-media-technology-2018/#vast-majority-of-teens-have-access-to-a-home-computer-or-smartphone

Anxiety and how to manage it: pre-teens and teenagers. (2022, October 19). Raising Children Network. https://raisingchildren.net.au/pre-teens/mental-health-physical-health/stress-anxiety-depression/anxiety

Anxiety in Teens is Rising: What's Going On? (n.d.). HealthyChildren.org. https://www.healthychildren.org/English/health-issues/conditions/emotional-problems/Pages/Anxiety-Disorders.aspx

Barnhill, J. W. (2024, January 25). *Specific phobias.* Merck Manuals Consumer Version. https://www.merckmanuals.com/home/mental-health-disorders/anxiety-and-stress-related-disorders/specific-phobias?autoredirectid=22113

Bilsen, J. (2018). Suicide and youth: risk factors. *Frontiers in Psychiatry, 9.* https://doi.org/10.3389/fpsyt.2018.00540

Boden, J. M., Fergusson, D. M., & Horwood, L. J. (2006). Anxiety disorders and suicidal behaviours in adolescence and young adulthood: findings from a longitudinal study. *Psychological Medicine,* 37(03), 431. https://doi.org/10.1017/s0033291706009147

Boystown. (2019, May 21). *What is a safety plan? When you need one and how to create it.* yourlifeyourvoice.org. https://www.yourlifeyourvoice.org/journalpages/safety-plan.pdf

Christina M. Cammarata, PhD. (2023, April). *About Teen Suicide.* Kidshealth.org. https://kidshealth.org/en/parents/suicide.html

Contributor, N. (2020, February 24). *How use of social media and social comparison affect mental health.* Nursing Times. https://www.nursingtimes.net/news/mental-health/how-use-of-social-media-and-social-comparison-affect-mental-health-24-02-2020/

Coronavirus Disease 2019. (n.d.). Centers for Disease Control and Prevention. https://www.cdc.gov/media/releases/2022/p0331-youth-mental-health-COVID-19.html#:~:text=According%20to%20the%20new%20data,hopeless%20during%20the%20past%20year

D'Amico, P. (2024a, January 3). *The relationship between teen Anxiety and Self-Harm*. Paradigm Treatment Center. https://paradigmtreatment.com/the-relationship-between-teen-anxiety-and-self-harm/

D'Amico, P. (2024b, January 5). *A Guide to Teen Self-Injury: Prevention, Signs, and Treatment*. Paradigm Treatment Center. https://paradigmtreatment.com/guide-teen-self-injury/

Denizet-Lewis, B. (2017, October 17). Why are more American teenagers than ever suffering from severe anxiety? *The New York Times*. https://www.nytimes.com/2017/10/11/magazine/why-are-more-american-teenagers-than-ever-suffering-from-severe-anxiety.html

Department of Health & Human Services. (n.d.). *Panic attack*. Better Health Channel. https://www.betterhealth.vic.gov.au/health/conditionsandtreatments/panic-attack

Elia, J. (2024a, January 29). *Generalized anxiety disorder in children and adolescents*. Merck Manuals Professional Edition. https://www.merckmanuals.com/professional/pediatrics/psychiatric-disorders-in-children-and-adolescents/generalized-anxiety-disorder-in-children-and-adolescents/?autoredirectid=21577

Elia, J. (2024b, January 29). *Obsessive-Compulsive Disorder (OCD) and related disorders in children and adolescents*. Merck Manuals Professional Edition. https://www.merckmanuals.com/professional/pediatrics/psychiatric-disorders-in-children-and-adolescents/obsessive-compulsive-disorder-ocd-and-related-disorders-in-children-and-adolescents/?autoredirectid=21577

Elia, J. (2024c, January 29). *Panic disorder in children and adolescents*. Merck Manuals Professional Edition. https://www.merckmanuals.com/professional/pediatrics/psychiatric-disorders-in-children-and-adolescents/panic-disorder-in-children-and-adolescents/?autoredirectid=21577

Elia, J. (2024d, January 29). *Separation anxiety disorder*. Merck Manuals Professional Edition. https://www.merckmanuals.com/professional/pediatrics/psychiatric-disorders-in-children-and-adolescents/separation-anxiety-disorder/?autoredirectid=21577

Evolve Adolescent Behavioral Health. (2023, September 15). *How do Adolescent DBT Programs Help Depressed and Anxious Teens?* Evolve.https://tinyurl.com/3f7x2jpj

Glasofer, D. R., PhD. (2024, January 16). *What is Acceptance and Commitment Therapy (ACT)?* Verywell Mind. https://www.verywellmind.com/acceptance-commitment-therapy-gad-1393175

How to support teens' mental health during COVID and beyond. (n.d.). Greater Good.

https://greatergood.berkeley.edu/article/item/how_to_support_teens_mental_health_during_covid_and_beyond

Jiang, S., & Ngien, A. (2020). The effects of Instagram use, social comparison, and Self-Esteem on social anxiety: a survey study in Singapore. *Social Media + Society*, 6(2), 205630512091248. https://doi.org/10.1177/2056305120912488

Keyes, M. A., Malone, S. M., Sharma, A. R., Iacono, W. G., & McGue, M. (2013). Risk of suicide attempt in adopted and nonadopted offspring. *Pediatrics*, 132(4), 639–646. https://doi.org/10.1542/peds.2012-3251

Lcsw, K. H. (2018, September 24). How to Parent a Teen That Self Harms. *psycom.net*. https://www.psycom.net/parent-a-teen-that-self-harms

Liz Nissim-Matheis, Ph.D. (2019, April 24). *The do's and don'ts of parenting an anxious teen*. Psychology Today. https://www.psychologytoday.com/us/blog/special-matters/201904/the-dos-and-don-ts-parenting-anxious-teen

Mars, B., Heron, J., Crane, C., Hawton, K., Kidger, J., Lewis, G., Macleod, J., Tilling, K., & Gunnell, D. (2014). Differences in risk factors for self-harm with and without suicidal intent: Findings from the ALSPAC cohort. *Journal of Affective Disorders*, 168, 407–414. https://doi.org/10.1016/j.jad.2014.07.009

Miller, C., Bubrick, J., PhD, & Anderson, D., PhD. (2023, January 5). *How anxiety affects teenagers*. Child Mind Institute. https://childmind.org/article/signs-of-anxiety-in-teenagers/

New CDC data illuminate youth mental health threats during the COVID-19 pandemic. (2022). *CDC.gov*. https://www.cdc.gov/media/releases/2022/p0331-youth-mental-health-covid-19.html#:~:text=According%20to%20the%20new%20data,hopeless%20during%20the%20past%20year

Pew Research Center. (2020, August 25). *Record shares of Americans have smartphones, home broadband*. https://www.pewresearch.org/fact-tank/2017/01/12/evolution-of-technology/

Smith, M., MA. (2024, January 8). *Anxiety in Children and Teens: A Parent's Guide*. HelpGuide.org. https://www.helpguide.org/articles/anxiety/anxiety-in-children-and-teens.htm

Social media and teen anxiety. (2017, December 15). Harvard Graduate School of Education. https://www.gse.harvard.edu/ideas/usable-knowledge/17/12/social-media-and-teen-anxiety

Staff, N. A. (2022, November 10). Acceptance and Commitment Therapy (ACT) for Teens: A Healthier way to cope. *Newport Academy*. https://www.newportacademy.com/resources/mental-health/act-for-teens/

Staff, N. A. (2023, November 13). New research on LGBTQ teen suicide rates. *Newport Academy*. https://www.newportacademy.com/resources/mental-health/lgbt-suicide-rates/

Staff, N. A. (2024, January 17). Social media comparison and teen mental health. *Newport Academy*. https://www.newportacademy.com/resources/empowering-teens/theory-of-social-comparison/

Suicide. (n.d.). National Institute of Mental Health (NIMH). https://www.nimh.nih.gov/health/statistics/suicide

Bibliography

Suicide rates among young people continue to rise, but there are ways to help. (2022, March 15). UCLA Health. https://connect.uclahealth.org/2022/03/15/suicide-rate-highest-among-teens-and-young-adults/#:~:text=Suicide%20is%20the%20second%2Dleading,National%20Alliance%20on%20Mental%20Illness

Susic, P. (2023, September 28). *18+ Teen & Kids Screen Time Statistics* (2024): *Avg. Screen Time for Teens vs. Recommendations*. HeadphonesAddict. https://headphonesaddict.com/teen-kids-screen-time-statistics/

Team, S., Team, S., & SingleCare. (2024, January 24). *Anxiety statistics* 2024. The Checkup. https://www.singlecare.com/blog/news/anxiety-statistics/

Teen suicide: What parents need to know. (2023, May 5). Mayo Clinic. https://www.mayoclinic.org/healthy-lifestyle/tween-and-teen-health/in-depth/teen-suicide/art-20044308

Teens and social media use: What's the impact? (2024, January 18). Mayo Clinic. https://www.mayoclinic.org/healthy-lifestyle/tween-and-teen-health/in-depth/teens-and-social-media-use/art-20474437#:~:text=A%202016%20study%20of%20more,levels%20of%20anxiety%20and%20depression.

Teens, Technology and Friendships | Pew Research Center. (2020, May 30). Pew Research Center: Internet, Science & Tech. https://www.pewresearch.org/internet/2015/08/06/teens-technology-and-friendships/

The Trevor Project. (n.d.). 2022 *National Survey on LGBTQ Youth Mental Health*. https://www.thetrevorproject.org/survey-2022/

The Trevor Project. (2024, January 9). *Facts about suicide among LGBTQ+ young people | The Trevor Project*. https://www.thetrevorproject.org/resources/article/facts-about-lgbtq-youth-suicide/

Twenge, J. M., Joiner, T. E., Rogers, M. L., & Martin, G. N. (2017). Increases in depressive Symptoms, Suicide-Related Outcomes, and suicide rates among U.S. adolescents after 2010 and links to increased new media screen time. *Clinical Psychological Science*, 6(1), 3–17. https://doi.org/10.1177/2167702617723376

Wall, D. (2021a, June 17). *Adolescent suicide*. ABCT - Association for Behavioral and Cognitive Therapies. https://www.abct.org/fact-sheets/adolescent-suicide/

Wall, D. (2021b, June 19). *Suicide*. ABCT - Association for Behavioral and Cognitive Therapies. https://www.abct.org/fact-sheets/suicide/

Wall, D. (2021c, June 19). *Ten steps to cope with the pandemic*. ABCT - Association for Behavioral and Cognitive Therapies. https://www.abct.org/fact-sheets/ten-steps-to-cope-with-the-pandemic/

Zhang, C., Leeming, E. M., Smith, P., Chung, P., Hagger, M. S., & Hayes, S. C. (2018). Acceptance and Commitment Therapy for Health Behavior Change: A Contextually-Driven Approach. *Frontiers in Psychology*, 8. https://doi.org/10.3389/fpsyg.2017.02350

www.ingramcontent.com/pod-product-compliance
Lightning Source LLC
LaVergne TN
LVHW040221110826
845146LV00005B/1368

* 9 7 9 8 9 8 8 4 1 7 3 5 4 *